YOU CAN BE A

POWERFUL

LEADER

Ivan W. Fitzwater

Ivan W. Fitzwater

6/10/81

MANDEL PUBLICATIONS
a division of the
Management Development Institute, Inc.
San Antonio, Texas

Library of Congress Catalog Card Number 78-55516
PRINTED IN THE UNITED STATES OF AMERICA
THIRD PRINTING
PRINTING BY SUMMIT PUBLISHING CO
SAN ANTONIO. TEXAS

AUTHOR'S INTRODUCTION

Leadership is an interesting phenomenon. I have spent a lifetime trying to attain it, and for the last fifteen years I have been practicing the art and science of teaching others the skills. The word "practicing" is used on purpose. Like other professions which operate in the gray area between proven facts and educated guesses, leadership training depends a great deal upon instinct and notions. I cannot precisely define what constitutes an effective leader, but I can recognize one in action, and I can help people be better leaders than they would be without training. That is about all of which I can be certain.

There are some axioms in the field of leadership which give structure to an otherwise enigmatic force:

1. **There will always be leaders.** No corporate undertaking of human beings can have direction unless there is a leader. This leadership can spring from the will of the group members in a very democratic way, or it may be usurped autocratically as by force. The point is that certain members, in some manner, will stand out in their influence on group activity. This is necessary to prevent chaos and provide survival.

2. **Vacuums of leadership are always temporary.** The explanation in item #1 demonstrates why there must be leaders. Therefore, when one person or group does not seek or grasp leadership, it is the same as assigning the opportunity to others. This is why an influential nation cannot withdraw from the world community without risking the leadership void being filled by an antagonistic force. The same is true of individuals in a club or organization who are reticent in giving up their share of power to those who are assertive.

3. **Leaders are the exception rather than the rule.** Most people seek the security of sameness which comes from imitating the actions, philosophies, dress, etc. of the majority. In this way, there is less chance of making a mistake and incurring the criticism or enmity of others. This is not really a bad situation when you think of it; only a few leaders are needed, so the competition is reduced. It is a hopeful situation for those of us who aspire to be leaders; while most are following followers, we have the law of averages on our side.

4. **All persons can profit from training if they want to be better leaders.** Note that I did not say everyone could be a great leader or even a good leader, but whatever the present level of attainment, it can be raised and enhanced. The better the raw material in such matters as appearance, attitude and education, the greater the potential for growth.

These accepted principles, along with pertinent knowledge of psychology and sociology, have not culminated in programs of leadership education by our universities. As a matter of fact, most leadership training occurs after the leader has somehow struggled up from the ranks. The armed forces and a few other forward-thinking organizations are among the exceptions to this generalization, but leadership education is still pretty much a seat-of-the-pants operation.

This book, then, is designed to help individuals who want to be leaders and organizations that want to develop leadership talent. I have experienced some situations which will help achieve this goal, and I respectfully present them here for your consideration and, I hope, approval and enjoyment.

Ivan W. Fitzwater

San Antonio, Texas
November, 1977

CONTENTS

CHAPTER 1

Mastering the Leadership Attitude

There is really very little difference in people, physically or intellectually. If several hundred people were gathered together in one room, their physical and intellectual abilities would fall predominantly in the average range. If an analysis were made of the accomplishments of these same people, however, we would find that a number of them would be leaders. They would hold positions of responsibility and prestigious title, but there would be no correlation between those who succeeded as leaders and those few who stood out physically and intellectually. In fact, it is common knowledge that persons with the highest degree of intelligence are not usually the ones who become leaders in business, industry and the professions.

Therefore, we must conclude from this that there is no correlation between a person's ability to achieve a leadership position and one who has superior intellect or great physical bearing. We must further conclude that human beings are more alike than different in innate ability, so we must ask ourselves: "What, then, is the difference? What causes some to be leaders and others followers?" The answer is obvious. The spark which causes some people to become leaders while others remain among the masses of followers is *attitude*. Those who for some reason are able to adopt and exhibit an attitude of leadership become leaders as a result.

Once this attitude of leadership is attained, the reaction of the world is quite predictable. The followers step aside and let the leaders assume authority; in fact, the followers help the leader achieve this goal. Think back upon some situation you have known in the past. When a group of people gathered together with no identifiable leader appointed or elected, what happened? Sooner or later, someone took charge and came forth with a plan, either preconceived or developed on the spur of the moment. The other people seemed gratified to have someone to follow, so they immediately adopted the plan as their own, accepted the self-appointed leader as their guide and then fell in line to help the plan become a reality.

Psychologists and others who work in the field of leadership development often use an exercise to demonstrate this phenomenon. A group of people will be gathered together during a seminar or training exercise. A problem has been assigned, but no instructions are given to any of them as to who will guide the group as they attack it. Copies of the problem or task are given to each of the group participants, and they are instructed to assemble in a certain room or place. At first there is a very uncomfortable air of tension as the participants look around to see who has been appointed to lead the problem-solving exercise. Nothing happens for a few minutes and the tension increases. Inevitably, someone will step forward and make a suggestion about what should be done to get the work started. It is not always the one who speaks first who becomes the ultimate leader, but once the ice is broken, it soon becomes apparent that one or several in the group have been thinking about what should be done in the situation. Once a suggestion is made as to how the work ought to progress or whether the group ought to go back to someone else for clarification, the others soon fall in line and accept the plan.

The point of the exercise is obvious. When there is no appointed leadership and a vacuum is created in this manner, those who have the propensity for assuming leadership will come forth and the stalemate or void is filled. Those with leadership potential cannot keep quiet for long, and those who have need for leaders feel a relief from the tension as someone steps forward to lead them.

What is Leadership?

The dictionary defines leadership as the capacity to guide or conduct, to influence or induce. The previous topic illustrated that this is not an inborn trait or inherited tendency. It is true that people who have certain characteristics such as height, physical bearing and good looks find it easier to assume positions of leadership. The real difference though, as has been demonstrated, is attitude; this comes about through a process of education which begins in the early years of life and is reinforced through environmental experiences. Perhaps it should be noted that leadership status can be given in other ways, such as in appointment to a position or an office, or through luck of birth, but effective leadership and the assumption of leadership in the absence of such artificial appointments come about through attitude. The epitome is reached when a person has advantageous physical characteristics supplemented by appropriate education and topped off by a positive attitude and a wholesome self-image.

Since by its very nature it only occurs in the human arena when one person affects other people, leadership can become a human problem. Although in itself leadership is neither good nor bad, history is full of situations where a person has been given a leadership role which resulted in terrible consequences to humanity. On the other hand, there are numerous instances where it served the common good. The definition does not rest upon the ultimate achievement attained, but whether one human being can move other human beings toward a goal.

Therefore, since leadership is ultimately the ability to influence other people to do something, the authority and controls exercised by the leader may be derived democratically or autocratically, and the force of leadership may be very subtle or an obvious one. The results attained are the final and only real measure of what has been accomplished by that leadership, and the proof is in the response of those who follow.

Traits of Successful Leaders

My experience in working with leaders over a number of years has led me to the conclusion that, by and large, they tend to exhibit certain similar characteristics. The list to follow is by no means exhaustive, but I think it is indicative of the common elements of behavior we can expect:

1. **A positive attitude which exhibits optimism and enthusiasm**
   Leaders see hope in even the most pessimistic situation. They are

the ones who pull the group out of the doldrums with a cheery word or other optimistic exhortation. They lead the cheers for the new goal to be reached even though it has been set higher than ever before. They want to set new records and seek competition because they believe they can make great accomplishments.

2. **An ego which needs satisfaction** A need to lead is a means of ego-satisfaction for the leader. This becomes obvious even in the most inconsequential setting or group as such a person consistently finds himself in a leadership role. Another way to say this might be that a leader finds it difficult to follow, particularly if another leader displays ineptness. This is why the person who spends all day in a position of leadership will also exhibit this tendency in his church school class, in a Little League meeting and in his civic club. This type of ego-satisfaction becomes an habitual need which remains with the person day in and day out.

3. **An understanding of human behavior** Leaders can "read" people to the point where they can use them to suit their own purposes. They know how to take advantage of the reticent, to deal with assertive personalities and to bring all humans with whom they have contact into harmony, or at least into an accommodating arrangement. They recognize that all people have their own individual needs, prejudices, fears, etc., and they know how to use these or minimize them in such a way that their own ends are served.

   A good example of this is in a selling situation. A salesman has to be a leader because he wants to cause another person to take action toward a preconceived end. He avoids stepping on the biases of a client and, playing up to the other's needs, he may use a form of flattery or admonition to move the person along toward his own goal, which is the sale of his product or service. He uses his instinct, knowledge and training to understand his client so that he will not make a mistake and, consequently, lose the sale.

4. **Effective communication** A leader can be charismatic, soothing and persuasive, or he can be blunt and unbending when the situation demands it. The point is that he knows how to convey his meaning to another person in a manner appropriate to his goal.

5. **Constant planning** Leaders want to get things done, and to do

4

so they must have a plan. It is not always a written plan or even a formal one thought out in advance, but the leader is always looking ahead beyond any given point in time. In other words, the leader is goal-oriented and always has in mind how a current activity ties in with future events.

6. **Ability to connect seemingly unrelated events** The leader can take situations which have no apparent connection, bringing them together to accomplish a new purpose. For example, a sales executive may recognize the need for certain goods or services in a particular sector of the economy; he also knows of a surplus or by-product in another sector which would fill that need, so he devises ways of bringing the two together to solve the problem.

One illustration of such creativity was reported recently in a newspaper. A large U.S. Army camp had a rule that soldiers could not enter local restaurants in their fatigues; therefore, soldiers did not eat out very often, particularly at lunch time, even though they were located very close to the center of town. A local restaurant owner recognized this situation as an opportunity, so he established a drive-in service area where soldiers could stay in their cars and still buy their lunches from his restaurant. After only a few weeks, there were seven hundred soldiers a day who were taking advantage of the innovation and the restaurant owner was making record profits. His creative mind took the two previously unrelated events and put them together to meet his own goal of making greater profits.

7. **Projection of an image of power** Leaders learn either through training or imitation that certain images are helpful to them. A firm handshake, steady mobility, calmness, forceful gaze, and a conservative appearance are among some of these power images. In other words, they do everything they can to show the world that they know where they are going and they avoid giving an impression that they are confused or not in complete control of their lives.

Negative Leadership Traits

In our attempt to understand the phenomenon of leadership, it might be well to cite characteristics which would not be indicative of an effective leader. The following twenty-five phrases denote characteristics **not** possessed by leaders. Some items are much more important than others, but a person having several of these traits will find it very difficult to exercise leadership and possessing a great number of them will find it virtually impossible.

1. Makes extensive use of cynicism and sarcasm
2. Frequently uses words like "adequate" and "status quo"
3. Is negative and defensive
4. Has an apologetic manner
5. Is a "buck-passer"
6. Is known as a procrastinator
7. Is intolerant and abrasive
8. Makes simple things seem complex
9. Has a poor personal image
10. Often seems in a quandry—lacks sense of direction
11. Finds strength in numbers—people and data
12. Often given to self-pity
13. Plays favorites
14. Has an aura of tension and nervousness
15. Is unpredictable
16. Is seldom punctual
17. Garbles communication
18. Has low sensitivity to needs of co-workers
19. Sets poor example in dress
20. Is known for pessimism
21. Evidences "workaholism" tendencies
22. Practices "scapegoatism"
23. Has a disorganized work space
24. Frequently shows anger
25. Has little sense of humor

Seven Steps to a Winning Attitude

We have discussed at some length what leadership is and what it is not. While our definition has not been precise, it is evident that certain behavior runs more of a chance of achieving success than other types. No matter what the level of current achievement in leadership, wherever you are on your road to becoming the type of leader you want to be, it is possible to accomplish growth. I believe the following seven steps can boost you along the way:

1. **We must be able to motivate ouselves and others.** Since there is very little difference between people physically and intellectually, it is obviously the highly motivated who stand out. Ordinary people who find some way to set themselves on fire with enthusiasm and zeal are the ones who climb the previously unconquered mountains, run the four-minute mile and achieve seven gold medals in a single Olympic contest, thus breaking all the previous records. William James, the father of modern psychology, pointed out that most people do not use over 5 per cent of their abilities. He said that if anyone found a way to use as much as 10 per cent, the world would call him a genius, but still he would just be an ordinary person who had found a way to motivate himself.

   I would suggest that one way to motivate ourselves and others is to set a very high goal. Small goals do not excite us or make it worth our while to make a really dedicated effort. A good example of this is the way that the United Way campaign has set new records for charitable giving in the United States. When people were left to their own designs as to the amount they should contribute to the United Way, only a modest level of giving was accomplished. In recent years, the United Way has adopted a program of setting goals that, at first, seemed beyond the ability of people to achieve. The result has been that the heightened goals have motivated people to do far more than they ever did before. The concept is a valid one. Setting a goal that seems almost beyond our ability to achieve brings forth our best efforts and causes us to do things heretofore believed to be impossible.

2. **We must overcome our stereotyped pictures of ourselves.** Stereotyping is usually very negative in that we tend to picture ourselves as not being able to do certain things rather than concentrating on what we can do. Sometimes it is due to a lack of courage. We tend to be fearful of trying something new.

   An illustration of this happened recently in a church school class which I attend. A woman was asked to get up in front of the congregation of the church on Sunday and make an appeal. She immediately replied that she was not able to stand up and talk in front of groups. This was obviously a negative stereo-typing of herself because she is able to stand and she is able to talk, and these are really the only elements necessary to get up and talk in front of a group. She had stereotyped herself because even though she possessed all of the characteristics necessary for performing the task of talking in front of a group, her image of herself was that she could not do this very thing.

The truth is that all of us could write a book or make speeches, learn a foreign language, perform mathematical computations and learn a new craft or skill. The reason that we do not do those things is because we have an image of ourselves that says that we cannot. Overcoming such negative stereotypes is essential for growth and progress.

3. **We must become better planners.** Someone once said: "To fail to plan is to plan to fail." We sometimes think that if we only worked harder everything would turn out all right. The truth is that it is not how hard we work that counts, it is how smart we work. A few moments spent in planning saves hours in execution. At the beginning of every year, every month, and every week we ought to clearly identify our goals which we hope to accomplish. This would keep us on a direct path and prevent us from wandering aimlessly in many directions.

4. **We need to recognize the uniqueness of the resource we call time.** Time is like no other resource at our disposal. We cannot store it, we cannot accelerate it, and if it is not used today it is gone forever. Each morning we are given 86,400 seconds; we either use them or lose them forever. We cannot rationalize by saying that others achieve more because they have more time. We all have the same amount and we all have all there is. The winning attitude recognizes and properly utilizes this unique resource.

5. **We must learn to persevere in our plans.** The winning leadership attitude is one that does not give up at the first setback. Every person is going to suffer defeats and adverse situations, but the leader is one who keeps on trying.

The famous story of the Nevada Comstock Lode illustrates this point. A man owned the whole area included in the part of western Nevada where these rich gold deposits are located. He worked his claim and found some gold, but one day when the sun was the hottest and his spirits the lowest he decided to give up and sell his claim. The man who bought it from him, in a very short time, struck the Comstock Lode which has yielded literally millions of dollars in gold. The first man could have had all of this if he had just persevered with his plan.

Perseverence is the mark of the winning attitude. The great inventions of the world are not made in a single day nor in one attempt; rather, they are the results of long years of dedicated effort in the laboratory, it is just that we rarely hear of the hundreds of failures which have occurred. Authors who write best sellers are usually people who have prepared a number of texts without ever having them published. The person who keeps trying runs a greater chance of having an outstanding success because most people will not persevere. The law of averages is just as true as the law of gravity. So, keep trying and your chances of success are greatly enchanced.

6. **We must be able to overcome adversity**. It has been said that "into every life a little rain will fall." The question is not whether we are going to have defeat, but how fast can we bounce back when it occurs. The winning attitude is one that never gives up but keeps on trying, even in the face of defeat.

The story is told of a young man who decided to make his fortune selling magazines across the United States. His work was going well until, in one small town, he met a young lady and fell deeply in love with her. He decided to stay there for awhile rather than move on, and soon felt the time was right to ask the young lady to marry him. He took her to a fine restaurant and bought a lavish dinner in preparation for "popping" the important question. When he asked her to marry him, much to his chagrin her response was negative. In fact, she said that if he were the last man in the world she would never consider marrying him. To illustrate how fast this young man was able to overcome adversity, we need only look at his response. With hardly a moment's hesitation he said to her, "Well, if you won't marry me, will you at least buy one of my magazines?" You see, he knew that the person who keeps on trying greatly increases his chance of winning. This is the attitude of a real leader.

Another good example is Abraham Lincoln, one of our greatest presidents. His life is a veritable litany of defeat until he was finally elected president in 1860. Listed among his failures are business bankruptcy in 1831, defeat running for the legislature in 1832, failure at business again in 1833, the death of his sweetheart in 1835, a nervous breakdown in 1836, defeat in the Congressional elections of 1843, 1846 and 1848, defeat when he ran for the Senate in 1855. He was defeated for vice president in 1856 and in the Senate race of 1858, but because of his ability to overcome adversity, eventually, he was twice elected president of the United States.

7. **We must believe in something beyond ourselves.** There are occasions in every life when we must be able to reach beyond ourselves and draw upon a reservoir of strength beyond human capability. For most people, this means a religious fortitude. It is imperative that the winning attitude have, as a strong foundation, belief in a Higher Being. This assures us that no setback or calamity of life can be so severe as to extinguish all hope. Even death itself is subjugated and placed into proper perspective when a person has faith in God. The following poem exemplifies my own thoughts on the need for such a winning attitude:

THE MARGIN OF VICTORY

Who decides what our fate will be
    when we play the game of life?
Who determines the final score,
    gives triumph, or merely strife?

Have the outcomes all been ordered?
    Are we puppets on a string,
Or does our Maker give a choice
    of results our life can bring?

No, winners have not been chosen
    but the rules have been firmly set:
We must decide what our score will be
    and the trophies we will get.

The world is a great arena for
    the one with a will to win.
Success and acclaim will surely come
    when we conquer defeat within.

> The difference is in our striving
> and what we think we can be:
> The will to win the game of life
> is the margin of victory.

The world-famous Olympic athlete Jesse Owens describes how he attained his dream of success. He said: "I built a ladder and this ladder had four rungs — one, determination; two, dedication; three, discipline; and four, attitude." I know of no better way to aptly describe how to be a winner.

CHAPTER 2

Exploiting the Phenomenon of Goals

There is not a person in the world who, if given the assignment of driving to a distant city, would just get in his car and start to drive . Instead, he would take the necessary time to plan a route which would take him to his destination. Without this planning, he might drive forever and never reach his goal. This example might seem ridiculous, but in the journey of life most people just keep driving harder and faster without any idea of a specific destination.

The same is true of daily tasks and larger jobs which we under-take. We usually have a general knowledge of what we want to do but the goal is too generalized to keep us from wasteful wandering. Just having a goal to "build a house" is not sufficient. We have to describe in detail the size and shape—give it specific dimensions. The only real differences between a dog house and a great mansion are the dimensions and specifications which illustrate the finished prod-uct. The architect, then, is really a goal-setter who gives detail to the dreams of the owner and sets targets of accomplishment which are specific.

Specific Goals vs. Generalized Statements

The effective leader must master the art of turning generalized goals into specific targets. It becomes standard practice to pin down in sharp detail the dimensions of the finished task. There are various ways of achieving this, but the simple, four-step approach to com-pleting any project is basic. This procedure can be used for a small job in the daily routine or for pursuing to completion a lifetime goal.

The difference is only in the magnitude of the task and the time frame for completion.

The Four-step Approach to Successful Goal Setting

Example #1   The Lifetime Goal

In stating lifetime goals, most people mention "enough money to live comfortably during retirement." This is certainly a commendable aim but not a sharply defined goal. How much is enough? The answer must be a sum of money—a specific dollar amount.

A study has to be made of projected living costs when retirement will begin and decisions must be made about a desired living standard and other anticipated financial obligations. Actuarial tables and average inflation rate tables are helpful. An *exact* dollar figure must be factually determined as the goal to complete step number one.

Step two involves establishment of a rational sequence of steps leading to the goal. This example is easy since the number of years to retirement can be readily determined, and dollar amounts plus compounded interest can be developed for any given number of years.

Step three is the time frame for reaching the goal. The number of years remaining before retirement is divided into the total amount. (Compounded interest is used here, too.) The person then knows how much must be saved each year, each month and even the next payday.

Step four is commitment to the plan. The goal is clear, the steps are determined and a time schedule developed. Personal motivation and flexibility in adjusting to unforeseen circumstances assure accomplishment.

Example #2   The Small Task

Smaller tasks can also suffer from generalized definition which results in insufficient clarity for proper goal achievement. To say our goal is, for instance, to paint our house gives some idea of what we hope to achieve but not the precise target; we need to plan for the most efficient completion and to prevent misunderstanding and misdirected effort.

Painting the house must be carefully defined so a plan of attack can be developed in a logical sequence. Mistakes, duplication of effort, and time loss will likely occur unless a complete definition of the project is provided. Instead of just "paint the house," a more usable statement of the goal would be:

1. caulk and seal all windows
2. replace defective boards
3. sand all rough spots
4. fill all cracks and crevices
5. apply a primer coat of paint
6. apply two additional coats of high quality latex paint
7. clean up shrubbery and ground area after painting

This gives a clear picture of what the job entails—the essence of step one of the four-step planning process. The goal is stated in terms of the outcome.

Step two, breaking the project into sequential steps, follows easily. Time allotments are then assigned to each sequential part in step three and all that is left is dedicated commitment to the plan, which comes in step four.

The beauty of the process is in its simplicity, the key being step one. A sharply defined picture of the finished product becomes a rifle target where wasted efforts which deter direct movement are cut away; it provides the straight line which is always the shortest distance.

High Goals Are Important

It is human nature to set goals just above the last achievement level. This is unfortunate because high goals provide the excitement necessary to motivate us and bring forth our best efforts. Since so little of human potential is ever tapped (ten to fifteen per cent in the opinion of most psychologists), fantastic achievement is possible for the person with outstanding desire. Olympic champions, great inventors and famous leaders are really average people who succeeded in motivating themselves.

Last year's sales results are a poor starting place for this year's goals unless we are willing to recognize how little was achieved compared to what was possible. An exciting, yet totally reachable, goal would be to double, triple or quadruple last year's sales. Little challenges bring forth little efforts; fortunately, for ambitious people the opposite is also true.

THE GOAL SETTER'S CHECK LIST

A. State the goal in outcome terms:
1. What will the finished product be?
2. Give dimensions, dollar amounts and quality statements.
3. Give complete details as to how it will operate, what will be done. Include all parts and phases.
4. Continue until all questions about the completed project can be answered with precision.

B. Break the task into sequential parts:
1. What is the logical order of progression; that is, what will be done first, second, third, etc.?
2. If more than one person is involved, how will the work of various people be coordinated to ensure meeting of deadlines and prevent conflict and overlapping of efforts?
3. Can any parts of the task be done concurrently to expedite the reaching of the goal?

C. Set a time schedule?
1. Start by setting a reasonable completion date for the entire project.
2. Set individual deadlines on each of the sequential parts.
3. Establish a monitoring system to ensure work completion and to improve adjustments which may become necessary.

D. Motivate all concerned and work with total commitment:
1. Visualize and state the exciting benefits which will be realized through completion of the goal.
2. Use group psychology to spur on everyone to his best efforts.
3. Hold periodic review sessions to generate continued enthusiasm.
4. Use progress charts and "thermometers" to record progress.
5. Give awards for exceeding interim goal steps.

CHAPTER 3

Using Power and Intimidation

Any person who is to succeed as a leader of other people must understand the uses of power and intimidation. This is true from the standpoints of both attack and defense. Capable leaders have to be able to use them and must recognize them when they are being used by others so they can counter and neutralize their effects. There will be no attempt made here to moralize upon whether they should be used. The point is that we must all be aware that they exist, that they are used consistently by all manner of people, and those who are in leadership roles must understand them if for no other reason than just to survive.

First of all, it is not necessary to gain influence or control by inspiring fears in our fellow humans in the contemporary definition of these terms. The power can be gently persuasive—the intimidation as subtle as subliminal suggestion. No one would condemn a championship tennis player who uses psychological, as well as physical, avenues to defeat his opponent—quite the contrary. We boast about the athlete who is able to identify his opponent's weaknesses and take advantage of them to win the contest. The same feeling is not always true about people in the business and professional world. An enterprising businessman who is able to amass a fortune through astute business dealings, the use of advertising and other techniques which appeal to people's weaknesses is often condemned for his success.

The question of ethics is relative. People use power and intimidation to achieve their goals for good or for bad, and it is almost impossible to influence human beings without understanding the techniques.

Some power plays are bold and obvious while others are subtle and very difficult to detect. A man who dominates a meeting by rising to the floor and shouting down other people is using an obvious power play. Far less obvious, but equally as effective, is when someone entices you to meet in *his* office rather than in your own or a neutral zone—the person who owns the office is in a powerful position when it comes to negotiation. Additionally, the man who makes a public offering for stock in a corporation so that he can gain a sufficient amount to take control is obviously exercising power. Another person may use skills of persuasion to get past the secretary who has been told not to admit salesmen. All of these examples illustrate the different uses of power to gain an objective.

There are literally thousands of possible power-play techniques. The attempt will be made here to give categories which are illustrative of types of power plays which can be employed.

Elevation and Height

It is not by accident that our judges are placed in the courtroom in positions above the audience. Height is a power indicator. This phenomenon has entered into our everyday language; we frequently talk about someone "looking down" on someone else. The fact that we have to look up to someone puts us in an inauspicious position no matter how minor the height difference may be.

If someone is standing up and talking to you to gain a power advantage, you can counter by also standing. If you notice you are in an office where a person is in a chair which is higher than yours and you have to look up to him as you talk, change seats or stand up yourself. If you are a short person, the power advantage which was given to other people can be minimized by dressing tall, using elevator shoes and compensating for the lack of height by taking positions during conversations and meetings which offset the natural height difference.

Emotions

Emotional power plays are probably the most frequently used. Anger, tears and jealousy are some which are used to gain advantage.

It's our policy not to take anything back after two weeks.

Fortunately, for every emotional power play there is an equally effective countermove.

For example, when someone becomes abusive during a conversation (and your natural tendency is to back away and give in), one technique which can be used is to lower your voice and speak very softly so that the angry person has to be more quiet to continue the dialogue. This is particularly effective when someone becomes hostile with you over the telephone. Just start whispering as you reply, and you will find that the other person's anger will be neutralized as he quiets down and strains to listen to your response.

"It's Our Policy"

A frequent power play used by commercial establishments and governmental organizations is the "it's our policy" excuse. For example, you return a defective item you have had for only a few weeks to the department store where you bought it. The salesperson says, "It's our policy not to take anything back after two weeks." The counter for that power play is simply to say, "Let me speak to the manager." If that does not work, you can then use the "Let me have the address of your corporate headquarters" response. Usually, this will resolve the situation in your favor.

Ego Appeals

In the advertising world particularly, intimidating tactics are directed toward our human weaknesses of greed, fear, shame and other ego-based feelings. Get-rich-quick schemes appeal to greed, deodorant commercials speak to our fear of being socially rejected, fund-raising schemes are based upon our feeling of shame if we do not give—all of which are ego-damaging feelings. The best way to counteract such maneuvers is to use common sense. No person would give you a get-rich-quick scheme if he himself were able to use it to his own benefit. All deodorants, if used properly, will protect you from being offensive. No one should feel ashamed if he has not met someone else's established quota of giving.

Social Pressure

This power play tries to make you believe that everybody else is doing something that, if you do not do the same, will make you an outcast. It is only another ploy used to placate that old insecurity of envy, and is, in reality, a means of imposing one's standards on another. Simply say to yourself, "I want to be me. If everybody in the world belonged to that one club and if everybody in the world drove that same type automobile, I could refuse to do both and still hold my head up high."

Incurred Debt

When you are given the red carpet treatment by someone other than a close personal friend, or when someone buys you a lunch or gift, you had better be ready to counter by thinking ahead to what this is going to cost you to pay off the debt. Usually, it means you are going to have to buy something you really did not want or return a favor that you would not ordinarily have done.

Time Pressure

If someone tries to coerce you into making a hasty decision or signing a document because "time is almost running out," it is usually a good idea to stop and say, "I'm sorry if I have caused you any trouble, but there is not sufficient time for me to be sure of myself in this situation." Do not sign anything or make a decision when someone is using the time-pressure power play.

Lawyer Power

If you are ever threatened with, "If you don't do [this or that], I will have my lawyer call you," an effective counter is to retort with, "Don't have your lawyer talk to me; have him talk to my lawyer." This usually neutralizes the power play and gets you back on an even basis.

These are only a few power plays which are commonly used every day in virtually every walk of life. A leader must be sensitive to such activities at all times. If someone mentions to you his connections in high places, this is an intimidator. If someone calls you by your first name when you really do not know him very well, this, too, is an intimidator. If you are negotiating a contract and the other party suggests that you meet in his office and he will have his people standing by to research any points or reproduce documents, he is using intimidation. To some people, the use of power and intimidation has become such second nature that they, themselves, do not realize it. It has simply become their method of operating.

You can use your knowledge of power and intimidation to protect yourself or to gain advantage over others. This is not a new phenomenon. You have been intimidating and intimidated throughout your life. Ask yourself why you live in the house and community in which you do, why you drive the type of car that you have and why you belong to the church and clubs to which you belong. It is probably not a question of the need for such choices, but the basis for such needs. The chances are that many of your decisions in life have been the results of intimidation rather than of vital necessity.

CHAPTER 4

Achieving Effective Communication

All human beings need to know how to communicate; leaders need to know it most of all. Those who have become proficient in the art and science of communication understand that there are really three phases to the act—the sender, the medium which is used and the receiver. The act cannot be considered complete and, certainly, communication cannot be effectively made unless all three elements are given proper consideration; here, truly, "the chain is only as strong as the weakest link."

The act of sending involves an idea or piece of information which is formulated in the mind of the sender. Here, at the outset, the message is clouded by his own interpretation of it. Even though he might think he is sending a perfectly clear one (he understands it!), it is already coded by such factors as the level of his communication skills, his current frame of mind, and his familiarity with the receiver.

A medium is chosen over which the message must travel. This can be a letter or other form of written communication, it can be in the use of sound waves for oral communication, or it might be visual, through the use of facial expressions and other kinds of body language. While traveling through the selected medium, the message is also vulnerable. Written communication falls victim to various interpretations of words and symbols as well as poor visual production and even complete breakdown if the statement is lost. Oral communication can suffer from poor hearing, from noise interference, or poor-quality sending such as with a highly-pitched, distracting voice. Visual transmissions, used alone or in conjunction with conversation, are lost completely in many situations.

Dinner will be ready when I darn well please,
and if you don't like it, you can eat somewhere else!

If the message survives the problems of dispatching and the method in which it is sent, there remains a further difficulty. Based upon his emotional and physical conditions, the person on the other end will proceed to translate it. Filtered through biases, preconceived notions and the momentary level of receptivity—a morass of obstacles—the message, as he perceives it, can be entirely different from the one which was sent.

Perhaps a simple example might illustrate this three-step process and how misunderstandings can occur: A husband sits reading his newspaper while listening to the evening news on television. He hears an announcement about a program which will be coming on in about an hour and he wants to be finished with dinner so he can watch the program. To get some clarification about the time schedule, he casually asks his wife when dinner will be ready. Having had her own problems during the day with nothing having gone right, the harried wife interprets his question to mean that he is pressuring her to hurry. Even then, the message might have been salvaged had the oven timer not gone off at the moment that he finished his question, so she has not heard the "Honey" which concluded his sending. She responds by telling her husband that dinner will be ready when she darn well pleases and if he doesn't like it he can go eat somewhere else. (Of course we all know that if the husband had preceded his question with, "Honey, there's a great program coming on in an hour . . .," she would not have misinterpreted the next part and the hurt feelings would not have occurred—on either side.) We can see, then, that the message was sent with one purpose, was garbled in the medium of sound, and was received through a decoder set on a completely different wavelength. What was sent and what was received really bear very little resemblance.

So it is that the effective leader must be able to control to a high degree the three elements of communication in order to gain the best transfer of information and ideas. He must be able to use good communication techniques orally and in writing, and he must be able to supplement the former with the proper body language.

Everything which is mentioned subsequently presupposes an adequate knowledge of grammar, spelling, punctuation and language mechanics. Indeed, one cannot become a capable leader if he has such deficiencies, and most organizations routinely screen their applicants for leadership positions by giving tests in these basics.

Defects must be eliminated through education and a great deal of practice in writing and speaking. Once this training is supplemented with skilled use of the dictionary, we are able to move toward improving the three basic areas of effective communication.

Oral Communication

In oral communication, the test is what is received in the mind of the listener. This is the only real test and is the evaluation used by the successful communicator. In this medium, it is important to speak clearly and to see the reaction of the listener. Techniques can be used to assess what is being received, such as asking a question or having him restate the message.

An exercise which is used in many communication seminars illustrates the importance of this point. The participants are organized in groups of two, given a topic to·discuss, then required to converse in the following way: one person makes a statement; before the second can respond or make another statement he must repeat the first person's statement. It is not surprising that in many cases what the listener receives is not what the speaker has sent.

Oral communication is enhanced by the quality of vocalization. A low, well-modulated voice is best. A highly pitched voice, a very loud one, or the constant use of trivial phrases such as, "and uh," "don't you see?" "do you follow me?" are all annoying to the listener. The loud talker may have a slight hearing problem. Speech therapy and voice training are certainly in order if speech defects are serious enough to affect one's oral ability.

Speech velocity is important, too. Talking so fast that the listener cannot keep up with what is being said is a waste of time. The speaker would be better advised to offer less information and make sure it is properly received rather than trying to cover too much. Here again, the guideline to follow is how much the listener can absorb with complete meaning, so it is better not to go on to a new idea until he has thoroughly understood the previous information.

Listening skills are essential. Effective listening means giving full attention to what is being said; it also means stopping the speaker at any time if the information is not clear. Questions like "Now did I understand you to say . . ." and "Is that what you meant?" can fill in

the gaps of misunderstanding. It is also important when partici-
pating in group listening never to talk with a neighbor during the
presentation. Not only does this detract from your own ability to
receive the message, but it distracts at least one other person and in
some cases a whole roomful of people.

When talking to large groups, such as in giving a speech, it is
important to make sure that everyone can hear and that the environment is free of distractions. A comfortable room away from exterior
windows with potential noises, a good audio system, and cooperation
from the audience are necessary for an effective speech. The speaker's obligations are to be sensitive to audience reaction, to have a
well-organized, interesting presentation and to honor the maxim that
brevity adds to any speech. Someone once observed: "The mind can
absorb only what the fanny can endure." How true.

The effective speaker knows his audience and his material. He has
planned well and rehearsed his presentation so that it is not stilted
and does not have to be read. He uses tasteful humor, not only to
capture the attention of the audience, but to intersperse levity
throughout the entire presentation.

A well-organized speech follows a three-step format which has
been used by successful speakers for many years. Specifically, tell
them what you are going to tell them, tell them, and, finally, tell
them what you told them. Stated another way, introduce the topic
briefly, fill in the details in a logical order and then summarize what
has been presented. This approach is certainly oversimplified but
basically valid in that it includes the elements most likely to accomplish understanding on the part of an audience.

Written Communication

The basic goal of written communication is to write to explain
and not to entertain, to present the message in a succinct style.
Ideas become garbled and unclear when flowery phrases and ambigu-
ous words are used to embellish a letter or memo. A better way is to
use simple sentences and the clearest words possible so that the medium does not take away from the intent.

Brevity is another good rule. Memos should be kept to one or
two paragraphs and letters should never go beyond one page. Some
of the most important messages the world has ever known have been

sent in an economy of words. The Ten Commandments, The Lord's Prayer, the Gettysburg Address are all examples of brief, but powerful, messages. The other extreme would be in the example of the bureaucrat who takes several hundred pages to describe how money may be spent in one small phase of a federal program.

It is always a good idea to give written communication a trial run. This can be done by re-reading a letter or memo an hour or so after writing it, keeping in mind the question: What would this mean if I were seeing it for the first time? If the communication is going to a group of people, it is probably worthwhile to have someone else read it and react to it before it is sent. The art of communication is so complex that the extra effort of a trial run is certainly justified, particularly if a large group of people is affected.

Proper sentence structure, spelling and punctuation were mentioned earlier as being very important foundations to any attempt at communication. It would be worthwhile to mention here that mechanics are also important when it comes to properly constructing a memorandum or letter. A memo should always be done in memorandum form. It should not, for example, include a complimentary close as is done in the case of a letter. The best advice is to keep from mixing memo and letter forms. When a letter is sent, there is always a salutation and always a complimentary close. The beginning and ending should set the tone as to whether the letter is informal or strictly business. If the salutation is "Dear Mr. Smith," the complimentary close should be "Very truly yours" or "Sincerely yours." If the salutation is "Dear Sam," the complimentary close might be simply "Sincerely" or "Cordially yours." A good, safe, middle-of-the-road approach is to use a formal salutation such as "Dear Mr. Smith," a semi-formal complimentary close such as "Sincerely" and sign the letter using only your first name. The full name of the writer should always be typed on the letter.

Body Language

Communication can be enhanced or diminished by the use of positive body language. An obviously attentive listener will learn more from the presenter; when the listener's attention is wandering or he is preoccupied, communication is weakened. The best posture for an effective listener is to sit attentively with eyes fixed on the speaker, with no distracting activities such as fumbling with papers or looking at a wrist watch.

Just as a firm handshake conveys interest in a person, so does visual attention. A quizzical look indicates lack of understanding or disagreement, and a faint smile of approval usually indicates the message is being received. Therefore, the effective communicator will always read his listener to make sure the desired result is being achieved, and the effective listener will make use of body language to alert the speaker as to how well he is coming across.

The public speaker must be constantly sensitive to the audience and its level of attention. When individuals start to squirm or otherwise become restive, he must be prepared to restate and conclude his message or to interject humor or some other device to bring them back into focus. It is virtually useless to continue when the body language of an audience indicates that the level of saturation has been reached.

CHECK LIST FOR EFFECTIVE COMMUNICATION

1. Oral presentations organized in advance
2. Memos and letters, brief and concise
3. Grammar, spelling, punctuation properly done
4. Consideration given to meeting place, audio system and total environment for large group communication
5. Good listening skills and habits practiced in daily communication
6. Voice well modulated and mannerisms eliminated
7. Good telephone skills used (get down to business quickly and end conversations politely without undue rambling)
8. Good quality reproduction of mass-produced written materials
9. Routine advance preparation for conferences and meetings
10. Well-developed sensitivity to group dynamics
11. Acute awareness of "body cues" in conferences and large meetings
12. Speeches and reports reflecting the "tell them what you're going to tell them, tell them, and tell them what you told them" process
13. Memos and letters done in proper form
14. Brevity emphasized in all communication efforts
15. Sensitivity to message received rather than to message sent

CHAPTER 5

Polishing Delegation Skills

A very significant aspect of leadership is the responsibility to delegate tasks to other people. The effective leader must recognize his obligation to properly assign tasks to those who work under him. In this way, his influence upon the entire organization is greatly magnified, increasing his own productivity as he works through other people. A good administrator realizes that he cannot do all of the things which must be done but, instead, must hold himself available for the higher level of managerial functions while others carry forth the daily routines of the organization.

This is not a selfish approach. It is essential in giving other people the experiences necessary for them to also move up the ladder of progression to greater responsibilities. In fact, proper delegation on the part of the leader will provide opportunities for a great number of people to increase their competencies and better prepare themselves. The leader who tries to do everything himself is not only fighting a losing battle but he is also denying his subordinates the opportunity which they need to gain managerial experience.

Lack of proficiency with regard to delegation will also place a limitation on the growth of an organization. Since growth and expansion are only possible beyond the limits of one person's ability to the extent that he learns to let others make decisions and take responsibility, the executive who insists on personally having a hand in all decisions and who is unwilling to let others take full responsibility for a portion of the operation automatically restricts the possibilities for growth of the organization. In addition, no matter how hard a person is willing to work, there is ultimately a limit to the span of control which he is able to exert. Not only is he choosing an early grave as a result of undue stress and overwork, but the person who insists on making every decision is restricting the possibilities of any enterprise.

What Hampers Good Delegation?

Since it is apparent that good delegation skills are essential to the growth and development of any company or organization, we must ask ourselves why we are not willing to authorize someone else to represent us. There is no simple answer, but some of the following facts might shed light on the problem. There are several natural and psychological phenomena which tend to mitigate delegation of authority and responsibility. The first is our unwillingness to think in global terms. Human beings are inherently self-centered, so we tend to think of all of our responsibilities as being personal ones. Since survival is the most basic of all instincts, there is a natural fear in giving away anything which is ours; because delegation of authority means that we give away a certain amount of power which we could hold to ourselves, we must learn to accept that condition if we are to successfully run a corporative endeavor of a magnitude larger than a single individual.

There is also the security which human beings find in detailed work. Most people start out at a level which involves routine paperwork and a follow-up of details. We were apparently successful in that position or we never would have been promoted to a higher responsibility. The fact that we did find success at this low level of assignment naturally causes us to retreat to routine work where our psyches will not be exposed to possible attack. A good example is the foreman who has been promoted due to his competence on the production line. The new assignment as foreman requires a higher level of decision-making and possible conflict with other people. When the going gets tough, there is a great temptation to go back and actually do the work on the production line where life was simpler and the contact was with things rather than with people. The things never talked back, never gave him a complicated problem; he easily was able to measure his success at the end of each day by the number of items produced. To overcome the security of detail work, we must realize that we have moved to a larger assignment and are now get-

ting paid a larger salary to deal with the more complicated tasks which are an integral part of management.

Another phenomenon which keeps us from being better delegators is the "do-it-better-myself" syndrome. Our selfish egos reveal our natural feeling of being able to accomplish something more adequately than any other person on earth. When approached logically, it is obvious that this feeling is not based on fact. There are really very few things in the world that we could do better ourselves if we were willing to give other people the opportunity. A good delegator must convince himself that he is willing to follow the precept that many people have the ability to do a particular job well if they are given sufficient authority, training and experience by doing.

Delegation Provides Incentive

The effective leader approaches his daily work by asking himself: What are the tasks which must be done by me? Any task so designated is then given a priority ranking so the executive can make the best use of his time. It is in the planning phase that the leader also asks the question: Could this task be done by someone else in the organization? If the answer is yes, then the job is placed in the group to be assigned to someone else.

The leader recognizes that delegating a task has no element of punishment nor is it passing on "dirty work" to other people. Quite the contrary is true. To do a task which could be delegated would rob someone of a chance to grow, have new experiences and prepare himself for promotion to higher levels of responsibility, so by reassigning these jobs the boss is expressing confidence in the employee and motivating him at the same time. Simultaneously, the executive is freeing himself for the more important tasks for which he is qualified.

People thrive on doing better work and as much as they can handle; it enhances their self-images and gives them the chance to use their innate, creative talents. The expression of trust inherent to good delegation skills is another way of saying to a human being, "I value you; you are important and I trust you." All of these are really expressions of the love and respect which all individuals need.

The proper approach to delegating is to relinquish the assignment completely. Ambitious and conscientious workers want to be given authority and assigned completed tasks. Once a common understanding has been reached as to what it entails and what will be accomplished when the work is complete, the subordinate should then be allowed to use his ingenuity and creativity to carry it through with a minimum of supervision. Oversupervision is an expression of distrust and lack of confidence. It also gives the employee a chance to blame anything that goes wrong on the boss who, really, has kept for himself the total decision-making responsibility. Workers say to themselves, either consciously or subconsciously: What's the use in my giving extra effort? He's going to get all of the credit anyway. I'll just do the least I can to get by and still hold onto my job. If this kind of situation occurs, work simply becomes an activity to gain a paycheck rather than an opportunity for self-expression and personal achievement.

Not allowing the subordinate sufficient latitude would also require him to return to the boss for approval of every interim decision, depriving the worker of the feeling of accomplishment once a task is completed and eliminating much of the natural motivation. A sense of personal achievement is possible when jobs have been properly delegated because the one completing the tasks knows that the success is the result of his own competence. He works hard because he knows he is either going to get the credit for a job well done or the blame for sloppy work and he prefers the former. Because he is not tied to someone else's time schedule or affected by someone else's lack of effort, he also has the freedom to accelerate his efforts. Here is an excellent opportunity where praise and recognition can be given for a job well done. The effective executive is quick to recognize the accomplishments of his subordinates and never tries to take credit for someone else's work.

Delegation also enhances accountability within the organization. Just as the subordinate receives full credit for the completed tasks well done, his responsibility for deadlines not met and work not properly completed must be accepted. The giving of authority to someone to handle an entire task is a double-edged sword. When it is done well, the person responsible gets the entire credit; when it is not, he should be held accountable. There can be no excuse to place blame on a group of individuals as there would be with shared responsibility.

What Should be Delegated?

Deciding what to delegate can be a problem, particularly if you have not been in the habit of using this management skill. The fundamental idea is to delegate anything which can possibly be done by someone else, keeping yourself available for visionary work such as planning and coordinating, thus preventing a "lid" from being placed on the organizational activities because the leader is spread to capacity. As a means of getting started with delegation, or perhaps as a refresher for those who are already doing this, let us review the types of activities which are likely candidates for delegation.

The first key word is repetition. If you find you have a number of activities which must be dealt with repeatedly, solve the problem once and then let someone else handle this task when it comes up in the future. In other words, develop the model solution and assign such tasks to someone else, applying that model every time a similar situation comes up.

Another key word is routine. A work assignment can be analyzed to find those things which could be identified as routine activities and which are not high on the scale of executive functions, since top management should address only the problems which are unusual or out of the ordinary. Probably repetitious in nature, they can be easily dealt with by clerical personnel rather than preoccupying the valuable time of the junior manager.

Anything which causes the executive to be overspecialized or underspecialized should also be considered as a candidate for delegation. For example, it would not be good business for top management to completely understand how the bookkeeping computer works. If the boss is having to get into data processing to this extent he would be much better off hiring a specialist to work with the computer, thereby freeing himself for management activities. The same is true for underspecialization. The executive who finds himself doing things that anybody can do is obviously not spending his time in the wisest way. This again stresses the point that leadership involves planning, problem solving and dealing with new situations as opposed to anything routine or of a repetitious nature.

What Should Not Be Delegated?

Since management involves goal-setting and coordination of various organizational segments toward the attainment of that goal, it is obvious that nothing should be delegated for which a goal cannot be determined. In other words, a task should not be assigned to someone else until the top manager and the person receiving the assignment agree exactly upon what the desired outcome will be. Example: The head of the company decides that an advertising program is necessary to help the growth of the company. The first step, and the one preliminary to giving the task to a subordinate, is to decide exactly what the advertising program should accomplish. Once this goal is set and agreed upon by both parties, then and only then can the subordinate be expected to put together a program which will meet the needs and satisfy the company head.

Disciplinary powers should never be delegated. It is true that subordinates can help with evaluations and ratings which result in subsequent disciplinary actions, but the power itself must not be delegated. Organizational harmony and efficiency can be maintained only when the person at the top has the final say in the matter.

Work should not be duplicated and delegated to individuals just to make them feel important. While effective delegation does have a motivational effect on subordinates, the motivational value is lost if it becomes apparent that the assignment was made for an ulterior purpose. It may also be a signal that the organization is over-staffed.

It is usually not wise for the executive officer to attempt to delegate the part of his job which would be termed "boardmanship." Boards of directors usually admire the executive who is a good delegator of appropriate tasks, but they expect the top executive to maintain a close relationship with them. Routine telephone calls, such as reminders of meetings and this sort of thing, can be done by lesser officers or clerical personnel, but major reports and recommendations should flow directly to the board from the chief executive.

CHECK LIST OF TYPICAL MATTERS TO BE DELEGATED

1. Attendance at meetings as your representative
2. Making speeches
3. Reading
4. Approval of requisitions
5. Letter-writing
6. Follow-up of deadlines
7. Reconciliation of accounts
8. Inspections and safety checks
9. Travel-planning
10. Office management
11. Appointment schedules
12. Bookkeeping functions
13. Proofreading
14. Personnel interviews
15. Trouble-shooting
16. Housekeeping chores
17. Maintenance and repair of equipment
18. Handling of complaints
19. Repetitive tasks
20. Clerical work
21. Talking to sales representatives

CHAPTER 6

Gaining Control of Time

If there is any one thing that distinguishes effective leaders from ordinary people, it is their ability to manage time. This stems from an appreciation and understanding of what time is really like. It is a unique resource—not like any other. When it comes to time, there are no rich or poor since all people have the same amount and everybody has all there is. It cannot be said that one person accomplishes so much more than another because he has more hours in the day. Both, obviously, have the same amount and the extent to which one succeeds in reference to another is largely dependent upon one's ability to deal with the uniqueness of the time resource.

Two executives in similar positions with similar responsibilities can behave distinctly differently depending upon each one's ability to manage time. One is always in a hurry, distraught because of impending deadlines and rushing to keep up with the next crisis in sight. Another person with the same responsibility seems to have a very quiet, controlled work situation and doesn't even seem to be in a hurry. The difference in the two situations really has nothing to do with the amount of time available, nor does it have anything to do with natural ability or physical strength of the two persons. The successful manager has recognized the self-defeating result of getting into panic and crisis. He has organized his life in such a way so as to be able to deal with the realities of his environment and he has taken steps to gain control of the situation and reduce it to a manageable, even pleasant, assignment.

It should be mentioned at the very outset that the term "time management" is a misnomer. No one can really control it. It was mentioned in Chapter 1 that time is like no other resource, and I would like to re-emphasize it here. It flows beyond the normal restrictions which can be placed on a resource. The 86,400 seconds given in each twenty-four-hour period are either used or lost. So, the decision must be made as to whether we shall use the time given to us today or forego it forever in the hope that the task we want to accomplish can be done within the framework of a future resource which we hope to realize.

The truth is that *there is time for everything we really want to do.* This is demonstrated in the lives of very active people who hold high posts and important jobs. They have developed an attitude which helps them meet their goals in life by controlling *themselves* in relation to time. They are able to set their goals and priorities and block out those things which would deter them from doing what they want to do with their lives. Time is actually lost when we lose control of that which is allotted to us, but the clock ticks away—at its evenly measured and ever-constant pace.

So, it all really boils down to the ability to plan. This is just as true in one's personal life as it is in the place where a person makes a living. For example, you will hear one man talk about all of the things he has to do at home—the garage needs cleaning out, trees need trimming, the leaking faucet needs repair and a whole collection of chores are not completed because he just cannot find the time to do them. Another person, because of his facility for planning, puts the chores on a list and disciplines himself to do them in order of priority and according to a schedule that fits his work and recreational schedule.

Some professors find time to write books, while others are always too busy. The difference is not in the teaching loads of the two professors, but in their ability to manage themselves in relation to time. The successful one has decided that writing a book is important. He has given it a priority assignment and planned it within his expenditure of time. Once this design for time usage has been established, it is much easier to attack the smaller parts which fit into the weekly and daily schedule. Writing a book is no longer awesome because the seemingly insurmountable task has been broken into little bites which are no longer intimidating. The technique of planning one's activities in relation to the constant time resource is the difference between success and failure. Indeed, it can be truthfully said that many times the difference between success and failure in the total life situation is really the ability to make the most productive use of time. Great proficiency in effective time usage is gained only through a minimum of training and much experience. The following topics should help any person who wants to gain control of his time be more effective in increasing productivity and reaching his goals at work and in his personal life:

Individual Time Analysis

The first step in improving our time management is to do an analysis of what is now happening to our time by keeping an individual log for a period of several days or a week. A review of the current situation allows us to find where we are duplicating our efforts, such as making several trips to the same place in a single day, or where we are overlapping with the assignments of another employee, such as our secretary. The amount of time we spend in meetings will stand out as we review the time expenditure summary. Realistically, we can expect to eliminate at least half of the meetings we are now holding, and we can reduce by 50 per cent the amount of time spent in the remaining meetings. This adjustment in itself would cut that time by 75 per cent, probably with no loss at all to ourselves or our organization.

This analysis also helps us to find our own individual time wasters. While it is true that many time-wasting activities are common to all people no matter what their position or assignment, it is also true that time wasting is a very individual thing and the best progress is made when we get away from the theoretical and start dealing with our own individual situation. For example, some people have a propensity for engaging in brag sessions or extended conversations not related to business. Someone else may find that his telephone calls are exceptionally long and can be reduced. Once a determination is made of what is wasting time for a given individual, then a personal program of time improvement can be developed to meet the individual needs of that person.

Timesavers work pretty much the same way. Depending upon our individual preferences and our type of work, we can select from a long list of potential timesavers those which will serve our own individual needs. Extensive study of delegation skills will not pay as much dividend for the housewife, for instance, as it will for the company executive. On the other hand, the housewife might find her situation greatly improved by taking a few moments each morning to develop a "to do" list. The point is simply this: the potential good to be derived from a long list of possible timesavers depends, to a large degree, upon the dictates of the particular individual's responsibilities.

Conquer the Crisis Atmosphere

It is enlightening to visit the office of two executives who have a similar assignment with comparable pressures and responsibilities. In one, there is a quiet atmosphere, free from tension, where work moves at an even and productive pace. In the other, everyone seems to be in a panic as people rush to meet deadlines and individuals find themselves in frequent conflict. The difference in the two situations cannot be attributed to anything except the attitude of those in authority who set the tone. It is that tone which can spill over into the remotest nooks and crannies of the entire organization.

The crisis atmosphere is not exclusive with business offices or work activities, however. Personal situations can also reflect the same phenomenon. We all know persons who constantly seem to be out of control of their lives. They have developed an ulcer-prone life style and they live it from morning until evening. This type of person usually gets up late, rushes through breakfast and leaves home just in time to hit the heaviest rush hour. Tension builds as he ducks in and out of lanes of traffic, trying to make up for lost time. In spite of all the rushing, he still arrives late for work.

Tardiness on the job means more tension and possible conflict; fellow workers resent this lack of respect for mutual obligations. The tension that an employee brings along to work is passed on to subordinates through a shortened temper and a generally negative outlook which has been developing, and the situation gets worse as haste turns into waste all day long. Little is accomplished, therefore, so that by evening the person goes home with guilt feelings brought on by lack of accomplishment, and regret for the interpersonal conflicts which marked the day.

By comparison, the organized person gets up in time to take care of all personal needs, enjoy a leisurely breakfast and depart for work with enough leeway to take care of any traffic crises which occur on the way. This preplanning assures early arrival and a chance for a few pleasantries before the day begins. The tension-free beginning continues through the day as deadlines are consistently met, thus producing a good feeling of accomplishment when it is time to go home. This second person recognizes the devastating effect which the crisis atmosphere can have on personal well-being and work accomplishment. Both persons have within their control the ability to make the difference between the two situations. External factors do not create or prevent the crisis atmosphere; the difference, as in most things having to do with time management, is in the attitude and performance of the individual.

Make Planning a Habit

Many people are surprised to find that planning is so much a part of an effective time management program, but it is truly the most important thing which can make the difference. The successful manager spends time at the beginning of each month, each week and each day identifying the major goals for accomplishment during the given period. Just bringing to mind these things which we want to accomplish keeps our goal in focus and moves us ahead with a minimum of wandering and wasted effort. Someone once remarked that to fail to plan is to plan to fail. It is also true that one minute spent in planning will probably save as much as an hour in execution. It therefore behooves us to start every day by taking a few minutes to look ahead into what we want to accomplish during that day. It is also equally helpful to spend the last few minutes at the end of the day looking ahead to the next day. In this way, our conscious and subconscious minds can sort out options and potential solutions to our problems, thus enabling quicker solutions than would be possible without any forethought. If there is any one mark of an effective leader, it is the constant emphasis he places upon planning; that is truly the distinguishing mark.

Maximize the Contributions of Subordinates

The key to increasing employee productivity and maximizing contributions of subordinates lies in effective delegation skills. This topic is dealt with in more detail elsewhere in the book, but it should be mentioned here under the heading of time management that proper delegation of duties is a basic timesaving technique. Additionally, subordinates' contributions will be enhanced by careful attention to proper training of employees, proper motivation and effective delegation on the part of the manager.

Training virtually speaks for itself. We can expect an employee to perform with a high level of efficiency only if he has been thoroughly trained for his assignment. This training should begin prior to initial service and continue as he moves on to assume ever greater responsibilities. It is also true that if a large number of mistakes seems to be showing up in the production effort, it is a signal for intensified training activities. Accountability also shows a large role in this total picture. The only way to eliminate a disproportionate number of errors due to carelessness is to make sure that employees are held accountable, which means the leader must be willing to face the unpleasant task of calling such a situation to the attention of subordinates. Although it should never be done in an angry or emotional way (we all make mistakes!), it is essential that every error be noticed and corrected so that it will not be continually repeated.

Motivation is often taken for granted, but it really should not be. The leader, by the very nature of his title, has the responsibility for the performance of other people. By gaining the total commitment of the workers through proper motivational activities, such performance can be enhanced. Incentive programs, encouragement and careful attention to recognizing competence will go a long way toward bringing results which best serve the organization and, at the same time, help the individual grow and prosper. Properly motivated employees are the greatest timesavers in any organization and undermotivated employees are the greatest time wasters.

Appropriate delegation also increases the contribution which can be made by subordinates. The key is for the leader to delegate complete jobs and give the subordinate an opportunity to act independently to complete the job. The manager must get himself thoroughly under control so that he is willing to give people authority to do their work; he must refrain from excessive control, causing a subordinate to return for approval of every small detail. Proper delegation involves giving the subordinate a clear view of what is to be done, assigning sufficient authority to carry forth the task, setting a deadline and accountability for accomplishment of the task at an acceptable level.

Interruptions Must Be Blocked

Throughout our workdays, we are constantly plagued with interruptions of our work schedule. The reason they occur with such frequency is that most of them look legitimate. A colleague sitting in our office talking with us would certainly look like a normal situation to any casual passer-by. The truth is that we may be talking about something that is totally unrelated to our work and really just be wasting time. Papers piled in the "in" basket would certainly seem legitimate since they achieved that status. Actually, many of these papers should have been thrown away as soon as they were received in the mail and never placed in the "in" basket at all. The telephone rings and we instinctively answer it. Out attention is taken away from the work at hand, and after we conclude the call we have to come back to the task, review what we had done before so that we gain sufficient understanding to go on to complete the job. Again we have been interrupted, but because it is the telephone we automatically assume it is legitimate. It may have been just a misdirected call or a very casual one which could have been handled later in a concentrated period devoted to telephoning. The list of potential interrupters goes on, but the basic concept is simply this—we have to determine whether the intruder is worthy of taking precedence over what we had really planned to do.

In the interest of effective time management, interruptions must be controlled. Casual visitors to your office must be screened by your secretary, telephone calls blocked and rerouted in a tactful way which does not detract from the objectives of the organization. Our colleagues must be brought to understand that we have time when they need it, but we do not seek constant interruptions. Techniques can be used to set aside time when visitors are encouraged to come in. In this way we group potential interruptions into a concentrated period and each one is kept short. For example, the school principal announces to the teachers that he is keeping a period from 3 to 4 p.m. set aside each day in case they need to see him. This is a polite and tactful way of announcing that his reception hours are

from three to four, and asking everybody to plan to see him during that time.

Times can also be established when all of the outgoing and incoming telephone calls are handled. Outgoing calls are a simple matter because we can merely group them into a concentrated period rather than interrupting ourselves periodically throughout the day. Grouping incoming calls is a little bit more difficult, but is possible with the cooperation and understanding of the secretary. She lets the caller know that her boss is not available now, but that he will return the call at a stated time. In this way, virtually all telephoning, incoming and outgoing, can be done in a shorter period and at a time that fits into the overall plan for the day.

Most basic to the handling of interruptions is, once again, the attitude of the leader. Many interruptions can be traced back to the ego needs of the person who is being interrupted. He thrives on a situation where people must come in and talk to him frequently because it massages his ego. He is the cause when subordinates come and check with him on every little detail of a job that should have been assigned and released. In addition, long social visits in his office go back to the fact that the boss, the biggest potential interrupter in the whole organization, keeps people there because he does not understand the simple technique necessary to conclude the conversation. No matter what the cause, if the analysis of time expenditure reveals a large number of interruptions during the day, coordinated action must be taken so that these unnecessary intrusions do not dissipate the most precious resource in any human endeavor—time.

Watch Out for Workaholism

It has been stated, and rightly so in my opinion, that workaholism kills more executives than any disease. The compulsive worker lets his time get out of hand as he spends long days at work with desk piled high, expending much energy but often accomplishing very little. When the truth is revealed, the workaholic is often running away from an unpleasant home situation or he is escaping into work because he does not have anything exciting to do with his leisure time. Most organizations have now recognized the truth about workaholism and they no longer encourage people to work extra long hours, but insist on people taking vacations and giving more attention to recreational pursuits.

President Jimmy Carter recognized this problem of workaholism when he issued a memorandum to his staff shortly after his inauguration. He ordered them to work reasonable hours and to devote time to their families and to avocational pursuits. Only time will tell whether he is able to live by his own dictates rather than becoming a slave to the flood of paperwork which will certainly inundate his office. I think it is significant that, traditionally, presidents of the United States, even with their great power and influence, have not been able to structure a reasonable workday and still be able to do everything that they consider essential. It is probably a good thing that we have mandated a maximum of eight years in the White House because it is unlikely that any human being could endure a period much longer and still maintain his physical and mental health.

Just as with any addiction or potentially fatal disease, workaholism has early indicators. Typical warning signals include the following:

1. You get edgy over a long weekend and are tempted to return to work.
2. You have eaten a meal and you suddenly realize you do not remember what you ate.
3. You always seem to be running caution lights at intersections.
4. Your temper is easily lost any time you have to wait in line.
5. Workdays gradually get longer with each additional year spent on the job.
6. Recreational and avocational activities are not a regular part of each week's schedule.
7. A thorough physical examination has not been taken within the last year.
8. Vacations are not taken on a regular basis or they are spent at home.
9. You have used work as an excuse to miss some very important events in the lives of family members.
10. On a regular basis, work is taken home to be completed.
11. You are becoming resentful of someone who you feel works less than you do.

The astute time manager recognizes that workaholism is not a productive example to follow. We need to judge ourselves and others on the amount of work we produce, not the amount of energy expended. The workaholic generally spends a lot of time at work, but he does not want to produce too much in terms of results because the job may run out. Reasonable time management dictates that we work, enjoy recreation and rest in a well-controlled cycle. In this way we can do the best job of all three—which are really basic elements for happiness and success. Any one of the indications mentioned above should be a danger sign, but if several of these negative elements are present, this should be a severe warning signal just as extremely elevated cholesterol is in the case of heart attacks.

A CHECK LIST OF TIMESAVERS

Use a uniform filing system
Write precise, clear, short memos
Employ good telephone skills
Delegate reading and letter-writing
Motivate employees
Develop good trash basket skills
Jot down ideas
Eliminate office, file and storage room clutter
Use a dictation machine
Employ a steady work tempo
Stress organizational goals
Double check appointments each morning
Make use of travel time for reading, listening, dictating
Telephone instead of traveling whenever possible
Rest regularly and completely
Speed read and skim
Avoid duplication of effort
Handle each piece of paper once

A CHECK LIST OF TIME WASTERS

Uncontrolled telephone
Poor delegation and methods of accountability
Too many meetings or meetings poorly done
Unclear communication
Failure to Plan
Perfectionism
Procrastination
Failure to say "no"
Poor self-discipline
Office clutter (including desk)
Excessive television-watching
Ulcer atmosphere
Poor office arrangement
Loss of temper
Disappearing without notice
Being late for anything
Blaming others for our mistakes
Poor sense of humor

CHAPTER 7

Coping
with Stress

There is a certain amount of stress in every organization, in fact in every life. This is not bad. Because a certain amount of it is necessary to keep us on our toes—to keep us motivated—stress can be productive. The real problem confronting us is the level of that stress. If it is at a wholesome one, then we get a lot done and overcome procrastination and natural laziness. When it reaches a very high level, however, it is neither comfortable nor a positive influence on our lives. The point where stress becomes DIStress is the danger point and the one which must be controlled.

As leaders, we are subjected to many more stressful situations than confront the average worker, so the real secret is to avoid the dangerous, destructive area of *distress*. It immobilizes us, and results in severe diminishing returns as we expend more energy to accomplish little or nothing because the situation has gone out of control. Physical maladies, irrational judgments, and trauma rob us of our ability to be successful leaders. To prevent this situation and keep our efforts productive and in a very positive vein, it is essential that we learn to live with the normal amount of stress which comes with leadership but that we learn to avoid distress. We must learn to follow certain policies in order to confine stress within acceptable limits.

Detachment

One of the best ways to deal with stress is to remember that the pressure of the job focuses on a position rather than an individual.

The superintendent of schools who receives many angry calls from disgruntled patrons learns to remember that these people are angry at the superintendent, not the individual who holds that position. This is a very positive thing, psychologically, because the individual can go home at night and sleep soundly knowing that the angry people are only venting their hostilities on the position. Decisions which aggravated these people were not made in his role as an individual but in his role as the leader of the school system. He did what needed to be done, and in any role as complicated as that of a public school superintendent there are a number of people who will be offended. This is natural, normal and, most important of all, unpreventable.

In this case, it is obvious that the stress which results is a perfectly normal condition and has nothing to do with the personality of the officeholder. Thus, the superintendent can detach himself from the problem and play the role only during normal working hours. A real problem will develop only if the individual who holds the job cannot detach himself from the role of leader. When the two become one and the same, then all attacks at the position become personal attacks and, therefore, filled with distress. The person who takes office problems home is destined to continue his stress twenty-four hours a day, inevitably leading to self-destruction.

Personal Organization

The individual who is personally well organized can do much to minimize the negative effects of stress. Rushing to meet deadlines, being late for appointments and lack of preparation for business obligations are all stress-causing factors, but good personal organization will minimize these and put them into proper perspective. Those people who have learned to conquer stress have a life style which is designed to prevent tension and a crisis atmosphere. Remaining composed and unperturbed, under even the most trying circumstances, does not have to be a façade of self-control; neither is it an accident—it is the result of good planning. For example, a person who gets up early in the morning so he can have a leisurely breakfast, take care of daily toilet habits and be ready to leave for work well in advance of any deadlines is a person who remains tension-free. He leaves home so that if a traffic delay is incurred he is not anxious because he has given himself additional time to take care of such emergencies. He arrives at work earlier than other people so he can begin the day in a leisurely manner.

A person who has not learned to prevent stress will get up late, rush through breakfast and dart in and out of traffic in an attempt to arrive at the office on time. This pressure leads to a very poor start; the tension derived from such a beginning carries through the entire day so that things get worse rather than better.

The same thing is true in regard to other obligations which must be met during the day. Someone with good personal organization leaves for appointments on time with leeway for potential emergencies. The disorganized person leaves late, comes in late to a meeting and has to apologize at the very outset. The old adage "Haste makes waste" is just as true as can be. The good leader learns not to over-extend himself and to keep everything under control. His office is well organized and orderly. The number of tasks he undertakes is within reasonable bounds. He works on one job at a time and he brings it to effective conclusion rather than doing a number of things at once but all them poorly. In summary, he consciously plans his time so that nothing in his life gets out of hand.

Listen to Your Conscience

The most amazing stress preventer in any human being is the conscience. If you think back upon your life, you will find that many times when you were under stress were times you had done things you really knew you were not supposed to do, and how tormented you felt as you waited and worried about the ultimate result of your actions. This is the real clue to stress prevention. The person who cheats on his income tax is destined to at least a couple of years of worry because of the threat of an audit. Each year, the Internal Revenue Service receives thousands of dollars of "conscious money" from people who were unable to live with their past actions of cheating on their income tax. The man who embezzles at the office also incurs for himself a constant threat of being found out, and thus is destined to a life of fear as he waits for the inevitable results of his indiscretion. Someone once said: "If you want to sleep well, the best recipe is to work hard and have a clear conscience." The price of indiscretion is inevitably distress. The wise person will learn to live according to a code of ethics and behavior which is acceptable to himself rather than incur the pressure which comes from violation of personal conscience.

Regular Diversion Essential

We learned as kids that "all work and no play makes Jack a dull boy." Someone has also proposed the opposite—that all play and no work makes Jack a dumb jerk." If work constitutes the entire life of an individual, distress is inevitable. Periodic change to a more relaxed activity is essential for a proper psychological orientation. Our most successful executives have learned that regular participation in a hobby, athletics, or other activities which have no relation to work, renews our energies so that we become more effective when we are actually working at our professions.

One of the fundamental rules for avoiding executive stress is to have vacations at regular intervals in order that we focus our minds and energies away from work so that it does not become all-consuming. Many organizations make it an absolute rule that regular vacations be taken. Since vacation means to vacate—to get away entirely for an extended period—it is not a good idea to try to take one in little spurts of a half-day here and a half-day there so that we continue to have our minds on our work. One point that is made in seminars which are designed to teach executives how to overcome stress is that leaves must be taken for a period of at least two weeks. Anything shorter than that seems to maintain the connection with everyday work and the desired result is not achieved. If every person took at least two weeks per year completely removed from the work to which he is normally assigned, he would probably be a more efficient worker when he returned and he would accomplish more during the remaining weeks.

Diversion, then, becomes a two-fold thing. The first is that we must regularly have short periods during which we pursue outside activities. Then, once a year, completely absenting ourselves from the office for an extended period will prepare us to be more productive when we return.

Determine Physical Condition

A good way to find the early warning signs of stress and keep it under control is to pay careful attention to physical indicators. A regular physical examination should be mandatory for every person who holds a responsible job. The sensitive physician can see the early warning signs of problems, recommending ways in which stress can be avoided. Such conditions as hypertension, being overweight and early signs of physical trauma will be apparent to your medical doctor. A thorough annual physical examination should be standard procedure.

One caution should be given at this point. Not all physicians are skilled in dealing with executive stress, but this should not be a reason for minimizing their contribution. The executive himself must understand that the results of a physical examination are essential data in planning his life style. Your mental health and your state of stress will be minimized when you have either a completely positive physical examination or when you have corrected any negative findings. The physician will report the results of the examination, but the executive must take it from there. If your doctor gives you a clean bill of health, all well and good, but anything which he finds wrong should be corrected immediately if maximum efficiency is to be maintained. The point is that it is up to the executive to follow through on whatever corrective measures the physician outlines. Do not leave it up to him to do everything; let him be the trouble-shooter and you be the corrector.

There is probably nothing more comforting and reassuring than the achievement of being in good physical condition. Conversely, when you are worried about a health condition you cannot attain maximum efficiency in your work. Make this a top priority—find out what your physical condition is and then correct whatever is wrong. The result will be a considerable lessening of tension.

Moderation In All Things

A real warning signal of extreme stress is overindulgence in such things as alcohol, tobacco and food. No attempt is made here to moralize upon whether drinking and smoking are good habits; the point is that when a person becomes reliant upon them, the situation is probably out of hand. For instance, many executives have been driven to alcoholism by stress, and many have attempted to alleviate their anxieties by escape into alcohol. Others, who may avoid alcohol and tobacco, consume excess amounts of rich, fattening foods as a means of forgetting their problems. None of these provides continued support for the executive; on the contrary, they become counterproductive since the escapes are only temporary. Just as a drug addict must increase his dosage to satisfy his craving, it is also true that alcohol and nicotine become addictive and, thus, only exacerbate the condition.

A good leader can indulge in alcohol, tobacco and rich foods to a moderate degree and find support for his activities. The key word is moderation. Any of these things taken to excess should be warning signals. Guidelines are hard to establish since every person is different, but a normal person can probably absorb no more than two drinks before dinner, one pack of cigarettes and 3,000 calories per day. I repeat, all of these must be adjusted according to the personality and life style of the individual. The essential thing to remember is that if drinking becomes more than a pleasant before-dinner activity, if consumption of cigarettes reaches the point of lighting one from the butt of another and weight goes beyond the normal limits established for a person's age and height, then these become dangerous signals of excessive stress. Drastic steps must be taken to get them under control and keep them under control, or problems will become severe and disastrous.

Watch Personal Relationships

When an analysis is made of the causes of tension and stress in the lives of many people, it is often revealed that they are not due to the direct obligations of work, but to personal relationships, and sometimes these personal relationships are not the ones at the office, but reflect conditions at home or in other places of human contact. Just as people are usually the solution to any situation, it is also true that people are generally the cause of problems. A person who is feeling stress must first ask himself: "How are my human relationships at home, at work and in the rest of the world?"

A good place to begin is to review the relationships at home. An unhappy marriage or conflict among other family members spills over into work and causes loss of efficiency which may, to the casual observer, seem to be a work problem. One might start by asking: "Would I be happy at work if things were happy at home?" To most people, the home is a refuge to which we can run when the rest of the world is unbearable. If this is not the case, then something must be done. We all need a haven to which we can retreat, be refreshed and refortify ourselves.

Although this treatise is not intended to get into domestic problems and their solutions, perhaps it is sufficient to say at this point that if there are problems at home, one should not live with the situation as if nothing can be done, but whatever action is necessary must be taken. It might mean counseling due to difficulties between a husband and wife, or it might mean a restructuring of time so that all family members have a chance to be together and, also, to discuss their mutual concerns. The family forms the foundation of the work of all of its individual members. Difficulty here will spill over into everyone's vocations, so steps must be taken to make the family the bedrock it was intended to be.

If stress is stemming from human relationships other than the home, the most likely place then is at work. It is rare that conflict in the church, the country club or other organizations becomes sufficient to bring on a state of anxiety. People should enjoy those with whom they work and they should find satisfaction in these personal contacts. If this is not the case, steps must be taken to improve the contacts so that they are pleasant and beneficial to the goals of the organization. In this situation, the best approach is a very direct one. If there is someone you are not getting along with at work you should engage him in conversation, seeking his cooperation to resolve the matter. If this is not successful, then you need to take steps to either change your situation so that you are not in contact with persons who are unpleasant to you, or if you are their superior you need to discharge them so there will not be a continuing source of friction.

In some cases, the executive may find that superiors in the organization are the source of the conflict. If this is the case and a direct confrontation does not resolve the situation, then one should consider changing employment. Just as there are many potential mates in the world with whom one person could be happy, there are also many organizations in which one could find success and fulfillment. It does not make sense to continue an unhappy relationship if it is not mutually beneficial.

Do What You Want To Do

A frequent cause of stress is the fact that people have to do tasks which they really do not like. It is not uncommon in an organization to find several people who are doing things they dislike intensely, but if exchanges were made among them, they could be responsible for tasks more amenable to each. Many executives continue to do things which are unpleasant to them when they could really delegate them to other people with no loss of efficiency.

One good way to attack stress and to make the work atmosphere more pleasant is to let other people do the things you do not enjoy. Since human beings are different, it is usually possible to apportion jobs among the people in the organization so that all will be doing what they like to do while making sure that all tasks will be covered.

There is also a larger question which a leader must ask himself: "Am I in the right spot for me?" At times, people will move up in an organization and find themselves reaping financial success but not really doing what they like to do—the college president who is in administration when he would really like to be teaching, the sales manager who misses his days on the road are two examples. Money cannot buy happiness, neither can it prevent nor negate stress. It is usually much better to be doing what makes you happy, and if that is in keeping with your moneymaking goals—fine; if it is not, you would be better off choosing happiness over money. When you DO make the choice (and you may be compelled to do just that), make sure that you do it according to *your* likes and desires. Many people are unhappy because they allow others to make these decisions for them. An ambitious wife or the president of an organization can place a man in a role where he is miserable.

Remember, our happiness is not only basic to *our* well-being but to those around us. We must not allow stressful situations to evolve into *dis*tressful ones. As successful leaders, we must never sacrifice our basic need for happiness and fulfillment by letting stress get a strangle hold on our lives.

CHECK LIST FOR COMBATING STRESS
(any "no" answer is a warning signal)

1. Are you doing the kind of work you most like to do?
2. Are your personal relationships at home and at work good ones?
3. Have you had a thorough physical examination with results showing no symptoms of stress?
4. Do you have your temper under control so that anger is a rare occurrence?
5. Do you feel younger than your actual years?
6. Do you normally sleep well, free from insomnia caused by worry?
7. If you indulge in tobacco or alcohol, is it done in moderation?
8. Do you maintain prudent eating habits?
9. Are you free of nervous habits such as nail biting?
10. Do you participate in a regular diversion such as a hobby or sport?
11. Are you able to concentrate on one thing at a time without being easily distracted?
12. Do you feel that your life situation is comfortably organized?
13. Are you able to take a long weekend without becoming edgy?
14. Do you regularly take vacations?
15. Do you usually clear the intersection before the traffic signal turns yellow?
16. After a meal, if you were asked, would you normally remember what you have eaten?

CHAPTER 8

Learning How to Say No

One of the most important skills for any person to master is the ability to say no in such a way that the desired results are achieved but no unnecessary negative results are incurred in the process. It is a skill which must be learned and, like other skills, performance improves with practice. An inability to say no causes us to overextend ourselves at work and in our private lives. This usually results in poor overall achievement, lack of success in the leadership role and perhaps most important of all, physical and mental stress and unhappiness. There are also situations where we must know how to say no to our subordinates or our children when we happen to be the ones in authority and decisions are a part of our responsibility.

"If you want something done, give it to a busy person." This cliché is very true, but there is also a "straw that [breaks] the camel's back." Well-organized and highly motivated people can take on a lot of tasks, but a close look at their success also reveals a keen sense of what is important. They choose what they do in keeping with their goals. They do a lot but they also filter out low-priority tasks which do not contribute to their goals. They decide what is important in life and "rifle in" on that rather than "shotgunning" their energies in all directions.

For example, the person who puts family in a high priority may have to say no to heading the United Way campaign, at least for a few years. The art of saying no emphasizes doing one task well rather than two things poorly.

My father once told me, "Prayers are always answered, but a great portion of the time the Lord says 'no.' " This illustrates our obligation as parents or as leaders in a business or professional organization. The obligation is incumbent upon us because we occupy a decision-making position. In any case, the ability to say no in an effective way is an important and productive skill.

Charley Sands was a highly successful insurance salesman. His ability, drive and the resulting success brought him a promotion to area manager and a move to a small, midwestern town. His big-fish-in-a-little-puddle status brought him requests to join and lead a multitude of organizations and projects. His church, civic clubs, professional associations and fraternal organizations all looked to Charley to head, not just one but, a variety of committees and projects. This caressed Charley's ego and he ran night and day to keep up with obligations, but this overextension of himself finally caught up with him—his work and family life suffered until a heart attack taught him how to say no.

Sally Weston wanted to be a good mother. Her status as a widow caused her to believe that extra firmness as evidenced by a curt "no" to every request by her children would make up for the lost father. The normal challenges of teen-agers turned into angry confrontations, and communication broke down altogether as Sally steeled her positions. The family she tried so hard to hold together disintegrated completely.

How can we learn when and how to say no effectively? How can we do what we must in terms of our available time and the obligation of our position without hurting others or communicating a lack of interest in their ideas or projects? The answer is not an easy one, but the ten cardinal rules which follow can help:

Ten Rules to Help You Know When and How to Say No

1. **Set priorities.** List those things which must be done (in keeping with obligations and lifetime goals) including a reasonable number of family and recreational pursuits. Then list, in priority order, other things which could be done if time were unlimited. Literally draw a line at a reasonable point and say no to all items below the line. This provides obvious justification for discarded items when you have to give a reason.

2. **Adopt guidelines well ahead of requests.** This will head off some questions and provide a basis for noes when they must be

given to subordinate workers or children. It is best if persons concerned are permitted to help establish the guidelines, thus minimizing conflict of values.

3. **Give reasons for saying no**. These don't have to be extensive, but plausible reasons soften the blow and show you really considered the question.

4. **Don't lie about why you are saying no**. Logical reasons are sufficient; you don't need anything beyond that. Besides, we usually get caught in our lies, anyway.

5. **Don't allow emotion to cloud the picture**. Arguments and anger aren't necessary. Don't let a simple no become "Hell, no!" by losing your temper.

6. **Listen attentively before you answer**. Everybody deserves a hearing, at the very least.

7. **Delegate decision-making as much as possible**. All noes don't have to come from you; don't do more than your share.

8. **Provide alternatives when possible**. The blow is softened if a kindred option is possible. Maybe the need can be met but in another way.

9. **Don't procrastinate**. When the data are in, make the decision. The problem won't go away, but it can fester.

10. **Reassess yourself**. Periodically review your priorities and base yeses and noes on the current situation. Don't let answers come from habit or outdated information.

CHAPTER 9

Dressing
with a Mission

There is abundant research to show that the dress and grooming of an individual have a very significant effect upon other people which can be either positive or negative, depending upon the individuals involved. What would serve the leader's purpose in one situation could be distinctly wrong with a different audience. The point is, it is important to consider what it is we are attempting to achieve by the way we dress.

Taste in clothing choices is a learned trait. It can be indicative of one's cultural background or native habitat—east, west, north, south, city, small town, affluent, modest—or merely family likes and dislikes. There is, however, a kind of uniform which has evolved that connotes success to observers. A rather neutral look, it usually categorizes the wearer as one who has "good taste," and, like the good manners we all learned as small children, is not exclusive to the privileged few. It is not necessary to be able to afford luxury fabrics custom-tailored in the latest style. The idea is to dress to achieve a purpose, not undo what we are attempting to achieve by detracting from our objectives through a negative appearance. That is not to say that we should become preoccupied with our wearing apparel. Low self-esteem or an attempt to disguise some deficiency are sometimes indicative of people who place undue emphasis on their appearance. Proper consideration, on the other hand, can give us an advantage in what we are attempting to achieve. To paraphrase Emerson: the way we dress speaks so loudly, it is sometimes hard for other people to hear what we are saying.

Generally speaking, appropriate dress for the most effective leadership image is the conservative type. Loud colors and patterns on an executive tend to give an appearance which engenders a negative image in other people. Some entertainers, and even some people in the business world, indulge in casual, bizarre dress; the public confidence in such types is very low. Bankers, lawyers and the clergy, who represent highly respected professions, wear more subdued styles which convey stability and conservatism. A person can take advantage of these attachments by wearing the uniform of one group or the other.

Older people, by virtue of their age, generally enjoy more public trust than younger people. Therefore, the younger executive needs to dress older; the older person who is trying to align himself with a younger clientele needs to dress young. This is not to say that there is no room for personal taste in the selection of clothing, accessories and grooming, but the wise leader will vary his uniform according to the needs of each situation. Careful study will reveal that professionals and management-level personnel have a uniform of dress almost as distinct as tradesmen.

The following check list illustrates some of the characteristics and considerations which the leader must bear in mind as he prepares to make decisions relative to dress and grooming:

CLOTHING

Fit and Style

Proper fitting of all items of apparel is extremely important. This does not mean that clothing has to be tailored if the person is able to wear standard sizes, but the clothing must hang properly on the body. Baggy pants, a collar too loose or too tight, a dress too far above the knee, pants legs too short or a shirttail that will not stay in create poor images. These may seem like very minor items, but they really are not. A man's necktie should reach just to the belt. His shirt sleeve should protrude one-half inch beyond the jacket sleeve. His shirttail should be long enough to stay in. In summary, every piece of apparel should neither be too large nor too small for the person. The man or woman who gains a few pounds or who loses weight should be sensitive to the need of adjusting clothing and have alterations made as necessary.

Quality of Clothing

It is not necessary to buy the most expensive clothing available, nor to have dresses and suits custom-made, to look smart. The important thing is to develop an eye in selecting clothing which looks flattering and fits well. Even the most expensive suit will look cheap if the lines do not meet properly at the shoulders and lapels or if the coat does not hang evenly. On the other hand, a relatively inexpensive suit will look good if a proper job of matching has been done by the tailor. When purchasing a suit, look for one of quality fabric or blend of fabrics which does not wrinkle easily and which will wear well for several years. Classically fashioned suits do not go out of style that quickly, but poorly blended fabrics will not stand up under the wear. Check, too, for firmly sewn, generous seams and other quality construction details.

Choice of Colors

Generally, the leader should go with subdued colors and gentle tones which are blended properly in the garment. Gray or dark blue pin-striped or muted plaid suits are the best for men who prefer patterns, and neutrals or quiet pastels or patterns are most suitable for women executives.

Cleaning and Pressing

No matter how much care is exercised in the selection of apparel, it will be to no avail unless cleaning and pressing are done at proper intervals. This is not to say that a suit has to be cleaned every time it is worn. It should be cleaned any time it is soiled and also periodically, since hidden stains can damage the fabric. The number of required cleanings and pressings can be minimized, however, if the clothing is properly cared for between wearings by frequent airings and the use of a hanger which retains creases and shapes. Since a suit's good looks are greatly affected by the sharpness of the crease, it should be pressed any time the crease diminishes even if cleaning is not necessary. (Never press soiled clothing, though, since the heat can permanently set stains.) Learn to clean up a small spot from an accidental food or drink spill as soon as possible. If it seems difficult to remove, get the garment to the cleaners quickly, with a note as to the offending substance.

Minor Items of Clothing

This is probably a misnomer, since there is really nothing that is unimportant when it comes to the total ensemble. A man's shirt or a woman's blouse must be chosen with careful thought. In fact, some of these so-called minor items can undo the total impact that is trying to be achieved. For example, a beige raincoat is generally more advisable than a black one because research has shown that beige has more of an image of success. Men's socks should always be long enough to extend to the calf and they should be of such quality that they never wrinkle. The color of the tie and socks should always be matched, and both should fit into the color and design of the suit. The design and color of shoes should fit all other items of clothing. Dark shoes with a minimum of design are usually best and the color must be compatible; e.g., black shoes do not match a dark brown suit and vice versa.

Accessories to the Wardrobe

Gaudiness in terms of rings, watches, eyeglasses, earrings, etc. is to be avoided. Pins or medallions which show allegiance to a particular group or cause should not be used unless one is assured that these will not be offensive to others not in sympathy with such a group. For men, heavy, dark-framed glasses, a modest gold watch and wedding band are about the limit. A college ring is all right if it is not too large and elaborate; however, several rings on one hand, though very stylish and even tastefully worn in some groups, do not convey an executive image for a woman any more than a flashy diamond of unusual design does for the male professional.

A briefcase normally may not be thought of as a clothing accessory, but indeed it can be. A well-constructed, plain, brown briefcase of medium size is usually best. It should show some wear because this is the look of success, but it should not be torn or otherwise be in need of repair.

GROOMING

Careful attention to what a person wears can be quickly undone if sufficient attention is not given to the important topic of grooming. A disheveled appearance which can come from the need of a haircut, a shave or perhaps perspiration spots on clothing creates the image of a person who is not in complete control of himself. Subconsciously, other people place him in a category with unsuccessful people and maybe even those who are to be distrusted. He would find it harder to get a check cashed or receive favorable treatment from a headwaiter or a ticket agent, and a sales representative in such condition would never gain admission to his client's office.

The few minutes that it takes to give sufficient attention to grooming will pay great dividends in the long run. This is particularly important for the person who wants to lead others, because any distraction from the impression the leader is trying to make will have a negative impact. The following comments relative to various phases of grooming give an idea of some of the concerns which must be addressed:

Hair

Here again, the emphasis is upon the conservative for both men and women. Moderate-length haircuts for men and subdued hairstyles for women are best. Wigs should be used by women only if they are well-tailored to the person's features and are not obviously artificial. Hairpieces are never appropriate for men unless they have been so well-fitted that they blend perfectly.

For a man, the haircut should be complete. This means that the hair should be shaved from the ear lobes and clipped from the nostrils. Psychologically, massive eyebrows can be a distinct mark of leadership so they need not be trimmed closely.

The use of hair dye is seldom in order and should never be used if it is obvious that the hair has been colored. Gray hair is a mark of distinction and leadership in men and, when properly cared for, in women. Moustaches and beards are still anti-leadership symbols, so have a negative affect upon other men. If it is the strong desire of a man to sport a moustache or a beard, it should be small and meticulously cared for.

If dandruff is a problem, an anti-dandruff shampoo should always be used since there is nothing more distracting than to see dandruff on a person's shoulders. A clean shave is also important and should be repeated before an evening engagement, particularly if a man has a dark or heavy stubble.

69

Deodorants

Even your best friend will not tell you if you have body odor, so it is better to take complete precautions and use an effective deodorant. Since human beings are oblivious to their own odors and the least amount of body odor can completely detract from the presentability of any human being, you cannot count on anything but prevention to keep you safe. Shoes, too, should be sprayed periodically since they will harbor odors. (This is particularly true for tennis shoes and other types of athletic footgear.)

Breath

Every person's breath has an unpleasant odor at some time or other. It should be an absolutely standard operating procedure to use a mouthwash in the morning and at other times during the day if breath might become a problem. Breath mints can be used before conferences or personal interviews.

Those who work very close to others during the day, such as dentists, physicians and barbers, should be especially careful.

Fingernails

Moderate length fingernails for women and fairly closely clipped nails for men are in order. It is imperative that fingernails always be clean. Dirty nails rank second only to bad breath when it comes to undoing the positive image of someone in a professional position.

Pipes, Cigars and Cigarettes

The complete absence of smoking material is becoming a real success image today. However, if a person does use tobacco the leadership symbols run in this order: the pipe is still the major symbol of trustworthiness and leadership, followed by small cigars with cigarettes running a distant third; large cigars still present an image of the carnival barker or con man.

Perfumes and Colognes

It is acceptable nowadays for men to use a subdued aftershave or cologne. Women can use more obvious perfumes, but they should be tasteful scents—not the overwhelming types for business use, anyway.

MORNING CHECK LIST FOR THE EXECUTIVE

Airline pilots go through a complete check list of items for each and every takeoff. They do this every time they fly even if the flights are relatively short and there are several in a single day. This repeated attention to details ensures maximum performance and accounts in large measure for the small number of airplane accidents. The same approach would pay great dividends for the executive who wants to make the best possible impression. A "preparation for takeoff" should be done every day so that nothing is overlooked or taken for granted due to the repetitive nature of getting ready for work.

Additional items may be added to suit individual taste, but at least this minimum list should be considered every morning, with most points adaptable to the female executive as well:

— 1. Shave (including hair on ears and nose hair clipped)
— 2. Hair combed in a natural look (no dandruff showing)
— 3. Deodorant liberally applied
— 4. Shoes shined
— 5. Fingernails clipped and cleaned
— 6. Suit sharply pressed
— 7. Mouthwash used
— 8. Shirt matched to suit
— 9. Tie and socks matched (socks at least over the calf and sturdy enough to stay unwrinkled)
— 10. Shirtsleeve showing at least one inch below jacket sleeve
— 11. Modest amount of cologne applied
— 12. Check of emblems or insignias which might offend
— 13. Beige raincoat if one may be needed
— 14. Dark-colored umbrella available
— 15. A smile on the face

CHAPTER 10

Increasing Employee Productivity

Motivated employees who are "on fire" with zeal for their work produce tremendous results; unmotivated employees watch the clock, take sick leave whenever possible and seek the security of groups antagonistic to management. It is a fact: production could be increased without additional personnel if a way were found to motivate an existing staff to a high level of dedication and effort. The company which decides to expand should consider the possibility of achieving the new production quotas by more effective utilization of the present staff rather than adding people.

Recently, I observed employees doing a similar production task in different companies in two areas of the United States. In the first, employees were paid a predetermined amount for each unit completed—in this case, fifty cents for each crate of fruit packed for shipping. Three hundred crates per day was the average completed per employee. This provided a good day's pay and the workers were happy because goal-seeking and subsequent goal mastery provided an exciting feeling of accomplishment.

In a different plant, the same task was performed but the rules were different. The contract set a limit of two hundred crates per day for each worker. (The two-hundred-crate workers had learned how to make packing two hundred crates take eight hours.) The difference in attitude was profound, with the latter employees sullen, grouchy and obviously unhappy. The first workers were motivated by salary incentive based upon effort; the second group received its pay based upon artificial goals which bore no relationship to effort. In fact, they would have been penalized and rejected by

72

fellow workers if they had produced more than the stated limit.

Our job as managers is to try to get each and every employee to work as if he or she owned the company. Here is an example which shows what I mean: I used to take my car to a very large garage for repairs. I never met the person who worked on my car—to him I was just a number. The result was shoddy work, no one who took a personal interest in me, no one who felt his personal reputation was at stake if I was not satisfied.

Now, I take my car to a small garage—a one-man operation where the owner-mechanic enjoys and takes pride in his life's work, and, because he is anxious for me to be pleased, he does a good job. He knows he can stay in business and make money only if he satisfies me and the rest of his small clientele. If this level of commitment and motivation were achieved in all organizations, a panacea would be reached.

Is it possible? Yes, in large measure if we use the right motivators to gain the commitment required. Then why do we not do a better job of motivating? I think it is because we do not understand the importance of motivation and how it can be used to achieve desired results.

We generally rely upon salary, job security and working conditions as our motivators. These work well if our employees are concerned about where the next meal is coming from, whether they will have a job tomorrow or whether working conditions are tolerable, but how many of your employees have these concerns? Probably not many. They have a steady job, money to acquire the necessities of life, and working conditions which are acceptable, if not ideal. Such motivators, however, will not produce much of an increase in effort if we are considering clerical, supervisory, management or executive personnel—the so-called white collar worker. This is not to say that lower than adequate salaries can be paid; remember, the fact that they have competitive salaries is assumed before we look for a higher level of motivators.

Psychologists tell us there is a group of motivational techniques which will be effective with employees who are already comfortable in terms of the basic necessities of life and competitive salaries. These are the ones to which we must look if we are going to increase the efforts of people at the management and executive level. We begin by determining the unmet needs of these employees, consider how we can satisfy them and, at the same time, gain greater effort from them. Remember, every person in the organization, including ourselves, is underutilized and capable of doing much more.

Basic Need #1: Achievement

Every person has an inherent desire to achieve something on his own. This need can be satisfied by giving an employee authority to carry forth a project independently so that when the work is completed the recognition goes to that individual and he feels the sense of increased worth. Very close supervision on our part is unwise because it takes away the motivation provided by individual achievement. Our challenge as leaders is to give people a job to do—the bigger, the better—and let them work independently to complete it so they can claim ownership of the successful results.

Basic Need #2: Self-actualization

We have an innate desire to do a job bigger than the one we are now doing. Management can capitalize on this by letting employees undertake more important jobs because work itself is a very positive motivator. Try this as an experiment: call in one of your workers and tell him or her that you are going to give him a task that is recognized as one with great importance. (Make sure that it is, of course.) See if it doesn't excite and stimulate him in a very positive way, and watch him launch forth with new vigor.

This approach works particularly well with secretaries. The boss who tells his secretary that he no longer wants to do the routine correspondence but is going to leave it to her from receipt of the letter right up to the point of his signature will find a more confident and happier co-worker. He will also find that a lot of work has been moved from his desk so that he has more time for executive tasks.

Basic Need #3: Self-esteem

All human beings have a need for praise. Think back to the last time you talked to one of your employees and complimented him on a job well done. After your conversation, did he then stop and decrease his efforts, or did he go on and work even harder because of the praise? My experience has been that efforts are greatly increased by a pat on the back. This means that every time we fail to praise one of our employees for a job well done we have overlooked a very important motivator. Even if we must change our own behavior or feel we are going out of our way, we must never again overlook good work. The manager who is always ready to criticize, who is never able to compliment, has his priorities upside-down.

Basic Need #4: Belonging

When we feel we are part of a team, we all work better and harder; thus, it behooves the executive to bring people together periodically to discuss the work ahead. In this way, all people have a chance to voice their opinions and suggestions and, more importantly, feel they have a part in the ultimate decision. None of us like to see things fail if we have had a hand in their development. The reverse is also true: if we feel we have not been a part of the decision-making process, then we feel little obligation to help the work succeed.

Basic Need #5: Growth

Employees who are systematically prepared to assume positions of greater responsibility automatically look ahead toward promotion and work hard to achieve it. If it is well understood in your company that those who work hard are the ones who get the promotions, this kind of attitude will permeate the organization. On the other hand, if promotions are given based on kinship to the boss or some other capricious criterion, the workers take a "why should I give any effort?" attitude since dedicated effort apparently is not going to be rewarded.

We can summarize by mentioning that motivated, highly productive employees are nurtured by individual attention. We in management need to talk to them, individually and in groups. We must learn about their aspirations; we must seek their suggestions and make them a part of the decision-making process. In this way, they feel they have an investment in the operation, as indeed they do, because as the organization succeeds, they succeed.

Management by threat, intimidation and coercion causes employees to look forward only to each paycheck, to get it with as little work as possible, and to be happy when the organization fails. We must prevent this by developing a team spirit where all people relish the success of the organization, where their personal goals mesh with the corporate endeavor, where they work as hard when the boss is away as when he is there.

Let me cite one example of how this atmosphere can be achieved: A real estate company in one of our southern states was doing quite well, but it was obvious that increased competition and general market conditions were going to require additional efforts to grow or even to maintain a top position in the industry. The owners, sensitive to what positive motivation might achieve, called together the sales personnel and other employees to discuss possibilities of future achievement. Excitement built as the entire group chose goals and sales quotas far beyond what management had envisioned. Everyone came away from the meeting with a sense of total commitment to these heightened goals.

Every day brought more excitement as all of the personnel in the organization gave the extra push to make the company succeed. Instead of adding new employees, which had once been considered so as to maintain the position of the company in the industry, sales were soon far beyond even the most optimistic expectations, and it was all done with the same work force which had been on duty during the previous period of years. Group planning, mutually developed goals, teamwork, and a feeling of belonging made a tremendous difference. It can work in any organization, the results being increased profits and happier, more efficient personnel.

CHAPTER 11

Choosing Successful Leaders

One of the most important tasks that any manager has is selecting those persons who will serve as junior leaders. It is not only a crucial consideration for the top person in the organization, however. The same obligation filters down through the various levels of responsibility. As the president must select competent vice presidents, so, also, must the executive secretary in any department choose suitable junior clerical personnel. Someone once remarked: "The answer is always people." Competent people do seem to make any organizational structure function with success and, conversely, ineffective people will not be successful no matter how well the organizational structure has been developed.

Leaders depend upon the performance of subordinates for their own success and, therefore, it logically follows that the selection of junior personnel is probably the most important decision that any manager ever makes. It is also true that the leader's continued success depends on his ability to make personnel changes as the need becomes evident. If he is not able to fire an unsuccessful performer, he is not destined to be a leader for very long. Forcing a change in personnel, particularly when it involves emotion, is never a pleasant thing to do, but it is an inescapable obligation that one assumes when the mantle of leadership is undertaken. This does not mean that one has to be arbitrary or unfair. In fact, quite the contrary is true. The evenhanded person who is known for his personnel decisions based upon facts and evidence of performance will gain long-term respect of all people, even those whom he finds necessary to demote.

Traditional Leadership Selection Criteria

No matter what the organization, there seem to be five basic reasons why people are selected for positions of leadership. They are normally listed as follows: ability, seniority, academic qualifications, legal technicalities, and government regulations. This list is given in no particular priority order because it varies from one situation to another. If a company is found to be in violation of federal equal opportunity laws, however, then these regulations would have predominance over all other considerations. When legal technicalities are present, such as the necessity of a license before promotion can be given, that could be a stumbling block for an otherwise qualified person. Assuming that these conditions are not present, then seniority is the most powerful consideration when decisions are made.

Bear in mind this is not what the top management in an organization would like to believe is true. Generally speaking, the boards of directors and the presidents will say that they promote people based on ability. They may even think that this is true, but formal and informal research on the part of many people who deal with all types of organizations clearly shows that seniority is the most common, overpowering criterion.

Ability and academic qualifications are usually rationalized to support the seniority decision. The same is true of in-house appointments. By far, the largest number of promotions are given to people who are already a part of the organization. Qualifications of the inside individual are often embellished to make him superior to those who are applying from outside. What is really happening is that the personal connections of the one already employed overcome superior qualifications of the person who is unknown. It is almost impossible to rule out the human consideration when it comes to selection of people. While it is understandable, and even admirable, that people have such feelings, it is also detrimental to the organization when someone with less possiblity for success is chosen for leadership over someone who does not have those same human connections.

The truth is that seniority is not a good reason to fill a vacancy. For one thing, the mere fact that someone has lived longer than another person is not a valid reason to assume that the older person has more knowledge or skill. It is also true that the number of years on the job is not a valid indication of accomplishment. A wise man once observed that an individual can have twenty-five years of experience or one year of experience repeated twenty-five times. We all know people who have worked at a job for a long time but have barely risen above the beginning level of knowledge and effectiveness. While familiarity with the operations of the organization under consideration might be beneficial, there is a labyrinth of human problems which are incurred when an insider is elevated to a position superior to the one previously held. It is hard to overcome the old relationships when one of the people who used to treat each other as peers is suddenly thrust above the rest. A case could be made in support of someone coming from the outside because he may have a better chance for success and provide a new opportunity to overcome past problems, which could haunt the future of someone appointed from the inside. When all emotional and legal considerations are brushed aside, it is the veritable truth that none of the criteria previously mentioned are guarantees of success in the new position. We need to look to a different way of selecting new leaders if we are to ensure the greatest probability of success.

Look for the Success Syndrome

By far, the most valid indication of future success is past success. On the surface it seems an oversimplification, but, like so many things in life, the simple concepts are the truest and make the most difference. These are the things of which clichés are made, but then most clichés have basis in fact. For example, another way of saying "a leopard doesn't change his spots" is: if you want to choose someone to be a future success, choose someone who has been a success in the past.

This does not mean that the new job and the old job have to be similar or even have anything in common. It also does not mean that the new position has to be an extension or a higher level of the old position. What it means is that success breeds success. Human beings assume a success syndrome, an attitude which carries over from one job assignment to another. If they don't have the skills necessary to the position, they find ways of learning them. They find the keys to successful accomplishment in whatever task they are given and they are not satisifed with anything less than a feeling of success.

Unfortunately, the reverse condition is also true. A person who is incompetent in his present position is more likely to be a failure at a new job assignment than someone in a neutral or successful spot. This does not mean that we are ever to give up on any human being, but it does mean that if we are trying to improve our likelihood of identifying future successes we must give consideration to past performance. Here is where many well-meaning people get themselves into difficulty as they make decisions about appointments. It is human nature, a very desirable trait, and a good thing to want to rehabilitate people, but unless you are willing to take a risk in the new situation, unless you are willing to realize that it is a rehabilitation set-up which is being established, do not try to use a new job to make a success out of an unsuccessful person. The odds are distinctly against it. The simple truth is that if you are looking for a successful salesman and your choice is between a successful carpenter and an unsuccessful salesman, your best bet, by far, is to hire the carpenter. The success instinct transcends most of the other criteria which could be used, including experience.

The leadership development programs of many large businesses and industries no longer give predominant emphasis to on-the-job experience. Instead, companies look at the traits of people who have been successful in the past and try to match them with people who are aspiring to the new positions. Sometimes these characteristics have little or no relation to the job; instead, it is a way of matching new people with those who have been successful in the past.

It is impossible to generalize because all jobs are different, but if you need a list of traits which would be considered essential in the selection of any leaders, the following would certainly be exemplary:

1. **Attitude**   The successful person has a positive attitude which sees possibilities for success in the future. To him or her, the world is a world of opportunity rather than a world of potential defeat.
2. **Optimism**   The successful person believes that situations can turn out all right. Realizing that things will occasionally go wrong, he feels that with reasonable effort the balance can be cast in favor of success.
3. **Enthusiasm**   Going about his work with eagerness and a positive

force, the successful person is not reluctant to undertake new possibilities nor is he reluctant to begin. He wants to get started and he is never one to drag his feet.

4. **Perseverence**   He is not one who gives up easily, but recognizes that the rewards in life are a direct result of the ability to "hang in there" until success is achieved. He has the knack of getting up one more time when he is knocked down.

5. **Ambition**   A good indication of the success syndrome is a natural ambition to get ahead. Not content to stay at his present level and continue to perform comfortably in that assignment from now on, he is always looking up to the next possible level of achievement.

6. **Self-initiative**   A true mark of a successful person is that he is a self-starter. It isn't necessary to spell out everything for him before he gets going. If anything, the success syndrome describes a person who is out ahead of his group because he is able to see new possibilities without having to be told of them.

7. **Judgment**   I don't know how you can teach judgment any more than you can infuse common sense into an individual. However, it is certainly true that a successful person possesses common sense and good judgment. To paraphrase Napoleon: if you have an energetic person who has poor judgment, shoot him immediately (metaphorically, of course). There is nothing worse than an aggressive person who lacks common sense.

8. **Personal Magnetism**   The ability to have a positive effect upon other human beings is definitely a necessity for success. A person who has difficulty relating to others and who cannot be accepted by them cannot make the connections which are necessary to properly influence other people. A naturally warm personality will carry anyone a long way toward making positive impressions upon other people.

Using Outside Selectors to Choose Leaders

It is virtually impossible to do an effective job selecting leaders within an organization without using outside consultants. There are just too many human factors which become involved in the selection process when it is done internally to retain the objectivity which is essential if proper decisions are to be made. Even if the organization is under new management, this is still true because of the fact that after the decisions are made, any emotional residue will still be attached to the new leadership. It is better to let someone from the outside implement an objective plan of management selection and then leave after the decisions have been made. This form of scapegoatism is perfectly defensible because when the outsider leaves he takes away much of the negative feeling which accompanies any promotion.

This is not to say that the organization is to lose any control over the selection process—quite the contrary. It is up to the board of directors or the other leaders to develop the job description and a complete set of specifications necessary for the person to be appointed. They describe the ideal person for the job, not in terms of an individual who might be available, but strictly in terms of the qualifications necessary for that position. Then the board or chief executive, or whoever is attempting to fill the position, steps aside and lets the outsider apply the process. Screening techniques, interviews, research into past performance, testing—anything that is necessary—are implemented by the consultant, who moves objectively through the process, ranks the several highest qualified candidates and, subsequently, submits his evaluation to the firm. Although under no obligation, if the task has been done with professional skill, the members are best advised to accept the recommendation.

One need reflect only for a few moments on the advantages of this system. The unsuccessful candidates can blame the scapegoat rather than the people with whom they may have been or are going to be working. The successful candidate feels that he got the position completely on merit rather than through any connections or other considerations. There are fewer wounds that need healing, fewer rumors of power plays and other surreptitious dealings and a generally more open and above-board atmosphere surrounding the whole selection process. The cost of such procedures is far less than the potential values to be gained; in fact, it may be quicker and cheaper to get someone who is an expert in the selection process to do the task rather than devoting the time of executives to a project about which they have little expertise.

CHECK LIST OF THINGS TO BE CONSIDERED
BEFORE AN APPOINTMENT IS MADE

1. How successful has the person been in past assignments?
2. Has he or she evidenced an interest in the new position and taken every opportunity to prepare for it?
3. Is he industrious and self-initiating?
4. Will the individual exhibit creativity in the new assignment, or just follow established patterns?
5. Is he willing to take the risk of leaving old, familiar job surroundings?
6. Will he create a positive image for the organization in the new assignment?
7. Is he basically a team worker?
8. What are the possible problems which might be created by the appointment of a given individual?
9. Is he adept at human relations?
10. Does he deserve the job based on past performance and behavior?

If the answer is no to several or even one of the above questions, it is probably best to leave the position open until you find someone who will give you a yes to every one of the questions.

CHAPTER 12

Making Meetings Count

Leaders need to be able to conduct effective meetings, and this means conscious effort must be put forth. Staff meetings, sales meetings, committee meetings, whatever the nomenclature, are usually poorly done. This lowers employee morale and squanders the most precious resource in any corporate endeavor—time.

The cost of meetings alone is enough to cause more than casual attention. Ten executives making $10 per hour in a two-hour meeting cost the company $200 in addition to the travel time incurred and the interruption to work flow which this demand appearance requires. This is not to say that meetings should never be called; instead, only productive meetings should be held and then only when the cost can be justified. Turning meaningless gatherings into productive sessions is an executive skill which can be learned if the leader is cognizant of what meetings can achieve when properly executed, and if he is aware of what poor meetings cost in terms of dollars and lessened employee motivation.

The typical staff meeting goes something like this: The group meets every Monday morning at nine o'clock. No one knows why either this day or this time is sacred; it "has just always been done." The truth is that the boss is normally late on Mondays, and this gives him a "buffer" (no obligations till nine) and a social occasion to ease into the week. He is not sensitive about being late and wasting everybody's time because—well, he's the boss.

Several employees come early and "shoot the bull" because nothing can get started in their shops until after the meeting anyway; besides, it is a good time to review the weekend football games over a cup of coffee. By nine o'clock almost everyone is there except the boss and two others who are not concerned because they know the boss never starts on time. At nine-fifteen the boss finally arrives and everyone is anxious to see what is going to be discussed. It does not really matter, though, because no one can possibly be prepared—the agenda is a mystery.

The boss begins his rambling diatribe and, just when he is getting organized, in comes the first of the late staff members. After painful and questionable excuses (seems the traffic was heavy—everybody knows he overslept), the boss starts over. Just when he has repeated everything he said before, in comes the second latecomer. A third repetition brings the time to nine-thirty. Nothing has been accomplished except that those who were on time have been punished for promptness. (Did you ever look at it that way?)

By ten-thirty, the meeting rambles to a close with nothing really accomplished except an announcement of another meeting the following Monday at nine o'clock. Cost: several hundred dollars plus demoralized employees, loss of respect for the boss, and loss of the most productive work time of the day. Additionally, junior executives tend to imitate the leader so that a chain of poor meetings filters down through the organization.

It does not have to be this way. The leader could have set a pattern of positive leadership by knowing and observing the ten cardinal rules for productive meetings:

1. **Always provide an agenda in advance.** Employees who know what is to be discussed come prepared psychologically and with needed data. They have also thought over alternative approaches to solutions of the problems.
2. **Prepare the meeting place.** A room is chosen where there will be no distractions to interrupt. Exterior windows are curtained and a sign is placed on the door indicating a meeting is in session, etc. The room temperature is set to prevent discomfort. Full attention to the work of the meeting is assured.
3. **Always start on time.** If employees realize that meetings always start on time, this attitude soon permeates the organization and it becomes standard operation. Just as erratic starts downgrade punctuality, consistently on-time beginnings become accepted and imitated.

4. **Set a time limit.** When the adjournment time is stated in advance, it keeps all participants sensitive to time and keeps the discussion on target. It is also helpful to set a time limit on each item on the agenda.

5. **State the purpose at the beginning.** Just as a production goal keeps everybody working toward a commonly accepted outcome, a statement of the meeting's purpose at the beginning keeps everybody aware of what is to be accomplished.

6. **Include only the appropriate people.** The list of attendants should be developed only after the agenda has been established. Calling people together by group titles (such as all directors or all sales personnel) should be avoided because some individuals may not be needed.

7. **Call meetings only when absolutely necessary.** Meetings can become social gatherings or ego-reinforcement activities. There is nothing wrong with social contact or pleasant conversation, but these activities should occur on personal time rather than on company time.

8. **Use meetings only when involvement of people is necessary.** It is a blatant waste of time to call people together to receive announcements or routine instructions. Unless an exchange of ideas and differing viewpoints need exposure, a memo is much more efficient and inexpensive.

9. **Practice good group dynamics.** Do not permit aggressive people to monopolize nor the shy to withdraw. A meeting is a group activity where viewpoints are synthesized. The leader must use techniques to control the verbose and to draw out the reticent.

10. **Use standup meetings whenever possible.** If a brief involvement of a few people is all that is required, call the group together in other than the standard meeting room. Just as an individual conference is shorter when you meet a person in the visiting area, a meeting is shortened when the participants stand.

These cardinal rules for more productive meetings will save time and money for the executive who is sensitive to the potential gain from good group interaction and the loss from poor interaction. These rules also reflect a positive attitude toward time as a unique and irretrievable resource. They can make the difference between profit and loss.

CHAPTER 13

Getting Ahead Faster

Successful leaders understand there is truth in the axiom: "To move up you've got to move out." This is another way of stating the fact that mobility toward the top is much slower if you stay with one organization or in one geographical area. Acceleration to top positions is enhanced if the leader is willing to move, and since a successful leader is always planning for his next step up the ladder of responsibility, this means that he must be willing to relocate himself to another part of the country. Ambition alone is not enough. One must be willing to undergo the trauma of selling a home; pulling the children out of school; perhaps leaving close relatives and life-long friends; changing churches, physicians, dentists and the whole gamut of familiar people, places and things. It is a difficult transition at best, and it will require the utmost cooperation of every family member. It can, however, become a positive element and a broadening experience if it is planned well and approached optimistically, while realizing an adjustment period will be necessary— the length depending upon the length of the move. This is the sacrifice which must be made in the name of success and the price which must be paid for quick promotion—essential if the top is to be attained in one lifetime.

Once all those involved in the transition accept mobility as the price to be paid for success and promotion, then the individual seeking advancement can move ahead to analyze the components which are necessary for a maximum level of responsibility.

Basically, there are three elements in the maximum upward movement:

Competence

To achieve a high level of responsibility and success as a top-level leader, one must have basic competence. This means a willingness to learn the skills in any given vocation or profession, a high level of formal training, and proven ability to accomplish the job. It may be possible to be assigned a high level of responsibility, but unless one has the competence to do the job and to hold it, such an assignment will be only temporary, so it is well for the leader to learn that continued success is not possible unless he is fully prepared. Hard work and the willingness to sacrifice in keeping with the value of the goal being sought is the only logical way. Anything short of this is delusion and no long-term success is possible, for there are no short cuts to competence.

Sponsorship

Once a person has reached a level of competence where he has salable skills which are in demand in the marketplace, the next thing which must be achieved is sponsorship. Somebody has to know that you have the skills, and they must be willing to put your name in contention for available jobs and assignments. In the professional world, this may mean bringing yourself to the attention of association executives through volunteer work at conventions and other meetings. It may mean going to professional placement services which are willing to showcase your skills and competencies in such a way that they come to the attention of persons wanting to hire executives. It may mean writing articles for professional journals or participation in workshops and seminars which bring together people from across either a large geographical area or the entire nation. The point is that some way must be found for people who are at the very top levels of business, industry and the professions to know about your work so that they can submit your name when a desirable opening occurs.

Visibility

One's light cannot be kept under a bushel if it is to be seen by those who are making decisions of selecting executive leadership.

Basic competency and sponsorship must lead to visibility which will put a person's professional wares in front of a large audience. On the one hand, there are many jobs which are open and which need to be filled by competent leaders. On the other hand, there are many individuals who have these very competencies, but need to be matched to the available positions. Visibility is the third segment of the triangle which brings all of these elements together. The aspiring leader who is sensitive to this triangle of promotion will build on the foundation of the competence and gain sponsorship through people of influence to gain the visibility which is necessary to landing the desired job.

If you study the profiles and backgrounds of successful people, you will find that they have been able to understand the triangle which is necessary for upward mobility and they have been astute in selecting those jobs which fit clearly into their overall lifetime goals. They know how to "toss their hat in the ring" for any given position, they know how to polish their resumé to fit the needs of the position, and they have studied other people who were successful in a similar situation. They prepare for the job interview by studying the biases and preferences of the interviewer. They know the needs of the organization and are able to speak directly to those needs. They make a positive impression in an interview by preparing themselves thoroughly in advance.

The result of such careful study and preparation is quick, upward mobility. Such individuals are able to achieve the "leap frog" effect by realizing that there is not enough time in one lifetime to go through all of the chairs from bottom to top in any given organization or profession. The people at the top did not go through all the chairs, and research into how they made their successes is invaluable. The top people have been willing to make the sacrifices which have been outlined above, and they have pursued proven methods of acceleration rather than staying in one place after they have mastered that particular job. The really successful leader is always looking ahead to the next possible promotion and is always looking for ways to "short-circuit" the system to speed up the process.

The things which we have been talking about here can be illustrated in this example: A young man finishes his professional preparation and goes to work for a leading bank in one of our large cities. He works his way up from the very beginning levels to the point of becoming an assistant vice president in one segment of the operation. He realizes that if he stays with this bank it will be at least fifteen or twenty years before he can reach a level just below president of the bank or possibly, with luck, of becoming president. He is not willing to spend this amount of time pursuing his goal because he realizes that he will be past middle age and an unlikely candidate for anything greater after that. Recognizing that he might be able to move faster if he relocates with another organization, he takes his training and experience and places it in the open market through his professional association and other contacts which he has made at this point in his career. By indicating his willingness to move, he is able to jump across many of the jobs which lie before him in his present situation and become vice president of another bank in another town. After a few years of success in this situation, he is then able to move to the presidency of a bank which is just being established. The new bank is looking for people with successful experience in the industry. In a matter of a few years, he has moved from the lowest professional level to the presidency by being willing to move. Once he has achieved bank presidency, he will be able, in a relatively short time, to move back, and, based on his successful experience, to the presidency of a larger bank.

This man has used the basic elements of competency, sponsorship and visibility, along with his willingness for mobility, to get to the top of his profession. Had he stayed in the original bank, in all probability, he would have moved one career step by this time with little likelihood of ever reaching his goal; by being willing to move, take chances, break old relationships, he is now the president of a large bank in an equal number of years. Career orientation, rather than geographical attachment, has been the deciding difference. A leader seeking top responsibility must detach himself from geographical orientation or he is destined to move slowly through the chairs with little chance of ever reaching the top.

A blueprint for a self-conducted "mini-seminar" on leadership skills development

Organizations grow and improve as their human resources are improved. This mini-seminar is designed to be a do-it-yourself training program for in-company leadership improvement.

The training can be done in a minimum amount of time, and can be led by any person who has familiarity with the concepts used. It is most effective when the seminar leader has been a participant in this particular training program, but this is not absolutely essential if the leader is willing to thoroughly prepare himself by reading the material in the book prior to beginning.

The transparencies can be prepared on film for use on an overhead projector or can be made into pages on a flip chart. The exercises and simulation activities should be duplicated and made available to the seminar participants so that each may have a copy.

Each transparency is preceded by directions for its usage. Each is designed to form the basis of a brief lecture by the leader and should be followed by group discussions, if feasible.

As with any training exercise, this seminar should be held in a room free from distractions, one with tables so the participants can take notes. Attention should be given to the fact that learners will need to see the material on the screen or flip chart. Breaks should be frequent enough to deter fatigue of group members; refreshments during breaks would also be helpful.

TRANSPARENCY 1

This transparency gives an overview of the material to be covered in the seminar. Rather than just read individual items or letting participants read them, it is well to put a cover over the projector so that one item at a time is revealed.

Some brief discussion on the part of the leader should be used to clarify individual items as they are shown. By the time the overview is completed, participants should be thoroughly aware of what will be discussed during the course of the program.

PURPOSES OF THE SEMINAR

TO UNDERSTAND THE MEANING OF LEADERSHIP
. . . HOW IT IS ATTAINED
. . . WHAT ARE THE UNIQUE ATTITUDES OF LEADERS

TO STUDY LEADERSHIP STYLES
. . . POWER IMAGES
. . . POWER USAGES, CREATIVE SELFISHNESS, INTIMIDATION
. . . AUTOCRACY, DEMOCRACY, LAISSEZ-FAIRE

TO EXPLORE WAYS OF DEVELOPING LEADERSHIP POTENTIAL
. . . RECIPES FOR SUCCESS
. . . SELLING, PROBLEM SOLVING, TIME MANAGEMENT
. . . DRESS WITH A PURPOSE

TO LEARN HOW TO COUNTER POWER USERS

TO SEE HOW WE CAN HARNESS OUR TALENTS TO SUCCEED IN
LIFE AND BE HAPPIER
. . . BUILD OUR POSITIVE LEADERSHIP TRAITS
. . . REMOVE OUR NEGATIVE TRAITS

TRANSPARENCY 2

An understanding of the derivation of leadership will help focus the discussion to follow. After giving the definition, it would be well to have members give examples of how leadership status is attained. Several examples of attainment through position, luck of birth, and effective learned skills should be beneficial.

The group should be asked to determine which of the three methods of attainment gives the best chance for ultimate leadership success.

WHAT DOES IT MEAN TO LEAD?

L E A D = TO GUIDE OR CONDUCT
TO PRECEDE
TO ALLURE OR ENTICE

HOW DO WE ACHIEVE LEADERSHIP STATUS?

OFFICE OR POSITION

LUCK
OF
BIRTH

EFFECTIVE LEARNED SKILLS

EXERCISE # 1

LEADERSHIP ATTITUDE INVENTORY

At this point each member of the group should individually take the test entitled LEADERSHIP ATTITUDE INVENTORY. When this is done, each question should be explained by the leader to see whether the participants gave the correct response in terms of the material in the seminar.

LEADERSHIP ATTITUDE INVENTORY

Encircle the best answer.

1. In a restaurant, a leader is more likely to sit with his back to a wall rather than in the open or with his back to the door . . . . agree   disagree

2. A leader would decorate his office in brilliant colors and have recognized master-pieces of art and sculpture rather than a neutral, subdued environment . . . . agree   disagree

3. A leader is more likely to dress according to his personal tastes rather than other considerations . . . . agree   disagree

4. Sitting with legs crossed is more a symbol of leadership than feet planted side-by-side on the floor . . . . agree   disagree

5. When the executive tells you to be seated in front of his desk rather than the conversation area of his office, you can usually expect bad news . . . agree   disagree

6. Intimidation is not effective in gaining advantage in selling . . . . agree   disagree

7. Maximum selling occurs when the salesman focuses his attention on the product . . . . agree   disagree

8. Offices should be arranged primarily for the comfort of guests . . . . agree   disagree

9. Feigned weakness or disability are ineffective as ploys to gain favored treatment from clerks, ticket agents, or work supervisors . . . . agree   disagree

10. The closer the supervision, the better a job is done by employees . . . . agree   disagree

11. Money is an effective motivator of people at the executive level . . . . agree   disagree

12. Democratic leadership means votes will be taken on major decisions . . . . agree   disagree

13. The time required to do a task can be dramatically changed by setting a deadline for completion . . . . . . agree   disagree

14. A problem can best be solved by going off to a private area just to think . . . . agree   disagree

15. A leader never "bluffs" in any situation . . . . agree   disagree

ANSWERS TO LEADERSHIP ATTITUDE INVENTORY

1. *Agree.* The leader sits in a way that causes his companion to focus on him and not be distracted by things which could be happening behind the leader's back if he were not sitting with his back to the wall.

2. *Disagree.* The wise leader decorates his office in a subdued way to keep from shifting attention from himself.

3. *Disagree.* The astute leader dresses with a purpose or mission.

4. *Disagree.* Feet planted firmly on the floor side by side give a better image of leadership than crossed legs.

5. *Disagree.* Bad news is usually given in a less formal conversational area than at the executive's desk.

6. *Disagree.* Intimidation is used frequently in selling.

7. *Disagree.* Maximum selling occurs when the salesman focuses on his client.

8. *Disagree.* Offices should be arranged to fulfill the mission of the office rather than primarily for comfort.

9. *Disagree.* Feigned weakness is quite effective in gaining advantage.

10. *Disagree.* The best job is done by employees when they are internally motivated.

11. *Disagree.* Money is not nearly the motivator as is satisfaction of the need for belonging, self-esteem, etc.

12. *Disagree.* Democratic leadership means faith in people; it has nothing to do with voting.

13. *Agree.* Deadlines tend to appreciably shorten the amount of time necessary to do a job.

14. *Disagree.* Problems can best be solved by reflections off other people.

15. *Disagree.* A leader often bluffs, but he knows the odds on the chance he is taking.

TRANSPARENCY 3

These fundamental truths about leadership should be presented and discussed. Initially, there may be group disagreement on some of these items, such as #5. It would be well to let the group continue the discussion rather than taking a strong stand in favor of the concept. It is likely that group consensus will agree with the statement when participants have had a chance to share observations.

FUNDAMENTAL TRUTHS ABOUT LEADERSHIP

1. SKILLS CAN BE LEARNED.

2. BASIC ABILITIES AND TALENTS CAN BE ENHANCED.

3. TECHNIQUES OF LEADERSHIP CAN BE USED FOR ACHIEVING PRE-VIOUSLY CHOSEN PURPOSES.

4. VACUUMS OF LEADERSHIP ARE ALWAYS TEMPORARY.

5. TRUE LEADERS ARE THE EXCEPTION, THUS THERE IS MINIMAL COMPETITION.

EXERCISE #2

WHAT DO YOU KNOW ABOUT YOURSELF?

Exercise #2 is another individual activity which should be done by each participant. The correct answers can then be read and discussed.

EXERCISE #2

WHAT DO YOU KNOW ABOUT YOURSELF?

1. The greatest differences between you and
   other human beings are:

   physical _____
   basic intelligence _____
   attitude _____

2. Your areas of strength and weakness
   are largely due to:

   heredity _____
   environment _____

3. There are only a few things you could
   not do if you tried hard enough.

   True _____
   False _____

4. Your success will depend to a great
   degree on how good a salesman you are.

   True _____
   False _____

5. Your life tends to be a self-fulfilling prophecy.

   True _____
   False _____

6. The percentage of natural ability you
   are now using is:

   90% or more _____
   60% - 90% _____
   40% - 60% _____
   30% - 40% _____
   15% - 30% _____
   less than 15% _____

7. With training and practice, you could run
   faster than 90% of people your age who do
   not train or practice.

   True _____
   False _____

8. If you are either an introvert or an extrovert,
   it is because you chose to be.

   True _____
   False _____

9. Much of your success or failure has
   been due to luck.

   True _____
   False _____

10. Your greatest chance for happiness and
    contentment will come when your major
    goals are accomplished.

    True _____
    False _____

1. Attitude; 2. Environment; 3. True; 4. True; 5. True; 6. Less than 15%; 7. True; 8. True; 9. False; 10. False

TRANPARENCY 4

The review of our attitude toward leadership is crucial to the success of the seminar. Sufficient time should be devoted to it to bring the group into consensus in support of the given statements. The poem, "The Margin of Victory," which appears in Chapter 1 of this book can be used to support these statements.

LEADERSHIP ATTITUDE

OUR ATTITUDE SHAPES OUR DESTINY.

POSITIVE BRINGS POSITIVE RESULTS;
NEGATIVE BRINGS NEGATIVE.

OUR ATTITUDE SHAPES THE WORLD
AROUND US: OUR ENVIRONMENT
RESPONDS TO OUR CUES.

ATTITUDE DETERMINES RESULTS —
GOOD OR BAD.

BELIEF IN SELF SHOWS, SHAPES RESULTS.

POSITIVE THINKERS MAKE UP A SMALL
PERCENTAGE OF THE POPULATION.

LAWS OF NATURE ARE THE
SAME FOR EVERYBODY; WE
DECIDE SUCCESS OR FAILURE.

LEADERSHIP ATTITUDE SAYS,
"I CAN, I WILL."

LAW OF AVERAGES IS AS TRUE AS LAW OF GRAVITY.

TRANSPARENCY 5

This transparency gets to the point of how to start building our leadership skills. Several examples should be given to support each of the six points.

It should be stressed that all of the actions taken must be sincere actions because falseness is soon discovered by those around us. For example, when we say: "Make everybody feel important," we mean to genuinely look for reasons to make people feel good about themselves. Additional illustrations which might be used include: (1) leadership comes when you decide what you want to do, then take whatever steps are necessary to make it happen and (2) successful leaders always get up once more than they are knocked down.

TO DEVELOP LEADERSHIP POTENTIAL

1. ACT OUT THE ROLE TO WHICH YOU ASPIRE.

2. TAKE ON A SUCCESS IMAGE.

3. BUILD YOURSELF IN THE EYES OF OTHERS.

4. MAKE EVERYBODY FEEL IMPORTANT.

5. DON'T COMPLAIN AND RATIONALIZE.

6. DEVELOP YOUR STRENGTHS; MINIMIZE WEAKNESSES.

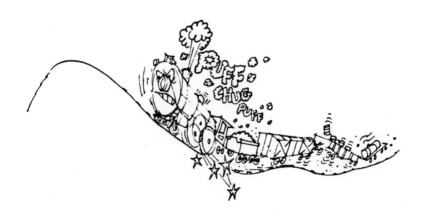

EXERCISE #3

HUMANOLOGY AND LEADERSHIP

Exercise #3 can be done as an individual exercise or in small groups. The fifteen items are designed to provoke thinking either on the part of an individual or a group.

In most cases the answer is not a firm "yes" or "no" but somewhere in between. Forcing the participants to choose either one should stimulate disagreement and thus foster productive exchanges between group members.

EXERCISE #3

HUMANOLOGY AND LEADERSHIP

1. People gossip primarily to hurt other people.

yes _____
no _____

2. Admission of a mistake causes loss of confidence by peers.

yes _____
no _____

3. Those who fail in business or in life in general do so because of lack of sufficient knowledge.

yes _____
no _____

4. The vast majority of people imitate leaders.

yes _____
no _____

5. Hard work gives the greatest assurance of success.

yes _____
no _____

6. People will be lazy workers if leaders fail to give them close supervision.

yes _____
no _____

7. Inherited abilities and weaknesses play a significant part in determining lifetime earning power.

yes _____
no _____

8. Anger is usually caused by frustration beyond the individual's control.

yes _____
no _____

9. Decisions made in everyday life are based more on emotions than facts.

yes _____
no _____

10. Great ability in a given subject in school usually comes from inherited characteristics.

yes _____
no _____

11. People resent spending time in group planning
and would rather have decisions made by a
strong leader.

yes _____

no _____

12. The most important element in teaching others
is to know yourself and your subject.

yes _____

no _____

13. Frequently asking others for help is a sign
of weakness on the part of a leader.

yes _____

no _____

14. Habits can make positive contributions
to a successful life.

yes _____

no _____

15. Learning to live with "skeletons in the
closet" is a challenge facing most people.

yes _____

no _____

ANSWERS

1. No
2. No
3. No
4. No
5. No
6. No
7. No
8. Yes
9. Yes
10. No
11. No
12. No
13. No
14. Yes
15. Yes

TRANSPARENCY 6

This is a listing of executive motivators in descending order of effectiveness. They really fall into two groups. The first group, which includes money, contract and working conditions, illustrates the techniques normally used. The remaining list shows those which would be most effective in working with people at the clerical, executive, and professional levels. These tend to be the motivators which are generally overlooked or taken for granted.

LEADERS NEED TO UNDERSTAND AND USE MOTIVATION

NEED	SATISFIER
FOOD, SHELTER	MONEY
JOB SECURITY	CONTRACT
SAFETY, PHYSIOLOGICAL	WORKING CONDITIONS
RESPONSIBILITY	ENLARGED JOB
ESTEEM	PRAISE
ACHIEVEMENT	AUTHORITY
LOVE	INVOLVEMENT
BELONGING	TEAM MEMBER
GROWTH	PROMOTION
RECOGNITION	INDEPENDENCE

TRANSPARENCY 7

This is a general discussion of what people are really like. It reemphasizes the idea that the positive approach must be taken by people in leadership roles. It also points out that human potential is virtually unlimited if we, as leaders, know how to bring out the best in our workers.

EFFECTIVE LEADERS UNDERSTAND HUMAN BEHAVIOR

BASIC TRUTHS

PEOPLE . . .

1. BASICALLY WANT TO SUCCEED

2. WORK HARDER AFTER EACH SUCCESS

3. ARE GOAL-SEEKING

4. GROW WHEN MOTIVATED

5. BECOME COMMITTED WHEN INVOLVED

6. WANT TO DO MORE AND BETTER WORK

ERRONEOUS ASSUMPTIONS

PEOPLE . . .

1. WANT TO AVOID WORK

2. WORK HARDER UNDER THREAT

3. NEED CONSTANT CONTROL

4. ENJOY AN EASY JOB

EVERY PERSON IS UNDERUTILIZED!!!

EXERCISE #4

This exercise is designed to have small groups of participants examine possible answers to the five questions. There are no correct or incorrect answers, and no two groups may give the same replies.

The idea is to require the participants to think about attributes of leaders and non-leaders.

EXERCISE #4

Discuss and attempt to reach consensus in response to the questions.

1. How do leaders communicate, orally and in writing, compared to non-leaders?

   _____

   _____

   _____

2. Is a leader's handshake, eye contact and touching different from a non-leader's? How?

   _____

   _____

   _____

3. What do effective leaders almost always do?

   _____

   _____

   _____

4. What do effective leaders almost never do?

   _____

   _____

   _____

5. Do leaders ever take unfair advantage of people? Can you cite an example?

   _____

   _____

   _____

TRANSPARENCY 8

This transparency reviews the images projected by typical leaders. The list of items should be reviewed with sufficient clarification given to gain understanding of each individual characteristic.

The five "power spaces" at the bottom of the transparency illustrate how the force of the leader is changed by virtue of location. For example, a leader in his own office is more powerful than the same person in a neutral zone, such as a reception area or conference room.

PROJECTING AN IMAGE OF POWER

STEADINESS, SLOW BUT SURE MOBILITY

CALMNESS, RELAXED DEMEANOR

FORCEFUL GAZE, PIERCING

LOW, WELL-MODULATED SPEECH

WELL-MANNERED, CONSERVATIVE APPEARANCE

THE LOOK OF HEALTH

A FIRM HANDSHAKE

PRIORITY FOR NAMES

CLEAN DESK, ORDERLY OFFICE

SPIRIT OF ENTHUSIASM

CONSTANT PLANNING

OBVIOUS TRUST OF CO-WORKERS

POWER SPACES

OFFICE AS A FORCE   NEUTRAL ZONES

PLACE AT THE MEETING TABLE

BUFFERS   PARTY STRATEGIES

TRANSPARENCY 9

The concept given here is to show that wholesome selfishness or "fair assertiveness" is not inherently bad.

The discussion should include the fact that we are born with instincts which protect us and cause us to reach out for opportunities, but these are often subdued by cultural training received at home and in the school. Some of the natural assertiveness needs to be reinstilled.

SELFISHNESS AND LEADERSHIP

EACH WIN IS A LOSS FOR SOMEBODY.

WHOLESOME SELFISHNESS IS ESSENTIAL TO SUCCESS.

EXAMPLES:

A.	PROMOTION	D.	CHEERLEADER
B.	TENNIS	E.	QUARTERBACK
C.	GET A BARGAIN	F.	PRESIDENT OF U.S.

MORAL QUESTION IS HOW TO BE FAIR *AND* SELFISH.

IN HUMANS, THE SURVIVAL INSTINCT IS STRONG, BUT REASONING, JUDGMENT AND CULTURAL CONDITIONING CAN MINIMIZE THE DRIVE.

WE ARE BORN WINNERS; WE LEARN TO BE LOSERS.

DON'T MISTAKE PASSIVENESS AS TACT AND COURTESY.

ASSERTIVE PERSONALITIES WIN.

TRANSPARENCIES 10 AND 11

These are illustrations of some normal power plays which are used by leaders. Directly across from each power play is a suggested countermove which can be used to neutralize the power play.

No attempt is made to moralize on whether the countermoves are fair; rather, attempt is made to acquaint group members with power plays which are used every day.

POWER-COUNTER PLAYS

POWER PLAY	COUNTER
ELEVATION	STAND, CHANGE SEATS, MOVE, DRESS TALL
SUDDEN ANGER	WHISPER
"IT'S OUR POLICY"	"MAY I SEE THE MANAGER?"

APPEALS TO:
  GREED
  FEAR
  SHAME
  EGO
	COMMON SENSE
	STUDY
	THINK

"SUCK-IN SELLING"	DON'T START LOOK AHEAD THINK TOTAL
BANDWAGON PROPAGANDA PEER PRESSURE	"I WANT TO BE ME."
IDOLS	THEY ARE JUST HUMAN

POWER-COUNTER PLAYS (CONTINUED)

POWER PLAY	COUNTER
RED CARPET	THINK DOLLARS
TIME PRESSURE	"SORRY I CAUSED YOU THE TROUBLE" – DON'T SIGN
LEGAL MAN	YOUR OWN LAWYER
UNANNOUNCED VISIT (WITH OR WITHOUT LEGAL MAN)	MAKE THEM WAIT
BROTHER-IN-LAW SELLING	I'LL BUY LATER
POLICE APPROACH	GET OUT, SHOW RESPECT
CREDIT COLLECTORS	KNOW THE LAW
CARBON COPY TO HIGHER-UPS	SEND REPLY CARBON TO HIGHER-UP

TRANSPARENCY 12

As is indicated by the title of this transparency, this is a general guide to the elements necessary for maximum success. Three items should be highlighted above the rest:

1. The importance of having a goal
2. The difference in people is attitude
3. Perseverence is essential for success (all people experience defeat)

RECIPE FOR SUCCESS

HAVE A DEFINED GOAL

. . . BE SPECIFIC
. . . DREAM A LITTLE
. . . MOTIVATE YOURSELF

REALIZE THAT SUCCESSFUL PEOPLE DECIDED TO SUCCEED
AND WORKED ACCORDINGLY

USE THE LAW OF ACHIEVEMENT

. . . REWARDS IN LIFE ARE BASED
ON OUR CONTRIBUTIONS.

. . . THE DIFFERENCE IN ACHIEVERS
AND NON-ACHIEVERS IS ATTITUDE.

USE THE BRAIN TO WORK SMARTER, MORE EFFICIENTLY, STAY ON
COURSE.

REALIZE THAT SUCCESS COMES AFTER REPEATED TRYING

. . . DON'T SELL OUT TOO SOON
. . . PUT DEFEAT BEHIND AS SOON AS POSSIBLE
. . . TOUGHEN THE EGO
. . . PRACTICE AND POLISH
. . . GET UP ONE MORE TIME THAN
KNOCKED DOWN

TRANSPARENCY 13

This is a discussion of things which potential leaders can do to make themselves stand out above the great majority of people. Emphasis should be placed upon the fact that this behavior is contrary to what is exhibited by most people, so conscious thought should be given to the necessity for being different.

AVOID GRAVITY-PULL OF THE MASSES

CHOOSE LEADERS
    AS YOUR IDOLS.

DON'T EMULATE THOSE AROUND YOU.
        ACCEPTANCE OF CONFORMITY OVERLOOKS OPPORTUNITY.

AVOID WORK AND
LEISURE RUTS.

TAKE A DIFFERENT
VIEW OF FREE TIME.

HAVE A PERSONAL READING PROGRAM.

RECONCILE ENERGY EXPENDITURES AND GOALS.

THINK

. . . OF NEW WAYS
. . . OF BETTER WAYS
. . . ANALYZE YOUR TIME EXPENDITURE
. . . MEDITATE

TRANSPARENCY 14

This is a general guideline for selling products or for selling ourselves. Definite emphasis is placed upon building rapport with the client and making contacts positive. Little mention is made of the product in selling ventures since this is of minimal importance compared to our image of ourselves and our knowledge of the client.

HOW CAN WE INFLUENCE PEOPLE?
(HOW CAN WE SELL?)

FIRST SELL OURSELVES

STUDY CLIENT OR AUDIENCE

HAVE RELIABLE DATA

BUILD THE STATUS OF THE BUYER

BE SINCERE

BE POSITIVE, AVOID NEGATIVE

BE HAPPY

PLAN AHEAD, BE ORGANIZED

LET NOTHING DETRACT FROM THE SUCCESS IMAGE

PERSONALIZE THE CONTACT BY KNOWING NAMES

LISTEN — LISTEN — LISTEN — LISTEN — LISTEN

TRANSPARENCIES 15 AND 16

The three common types of leadership philosophy are explored in detail. Autocratic leadership, as demonstrated in the first transparency, will do for a short period of time but does not have lasting value.

TYPES OF LEADERSHIP

AUTOCRATIC

. . . DOMINATES, DIRECTS

. . . DECIDES ALL ISSUES

. . . ENCOURAGES NO PARTICIPATION IN PLANNING OR CONTROL BY
NUMBERS

. . . MAKES PERSONAL CRITICISMS

. . . ASSUMES ALL RESPONSIBILITY

. . . MAINTAINS WIDE SOCIAL DISTANCE FROM MEMBERS

. . . DEFINES GOALS, IMPOSES THEM ON MEMBERS

. . . INITIATES ALL ACTIVITY

Laissez-faire leadership, as its name implies, is actually the absence of leadership. Democratic leadership is by far the most beneficial in achieving mutual goals.

LAISSEZ-FAIRE

OPERATES AS "OBSERVER"

MAKES NO ATTEMPT TO REGULATE OR ORIENT

ALLOWS COMPLETE MEMBER FREEDOM — NO RESTRICTIONS IMPOSED ON MEMBERS — NO CLEAR GOALS ESTABLISHED

ALLOWS COMPLETE NONPARTICIPATION, NO PARTICIPATION OF LEADER WITH GROUP

DEMOCRATIC

SHARES CONTROL WITH MEMBERS

ASKS FOR CONTRIBUTIONS

MAKES OBJECTIVE CRITICISMS

ENCOURAGES GROUP INITIATIVE

DELEGATES RESPONSIBILITY

PARTICIPATES IN ACTIVITY

HAS CLOSE RELATIONSHIPS WITH MEMBERS

ESTABLISHES MUTUAL GOALS

TRANSPARENCY 17

This is a general review of time management as it relates to executive leadership. The items in the list all require extensive interpretation. Because of the amount of material which could be covered in connection with these items, it is preferable to have the leader cover this in a lecture rather than attempt to discover the meaning of the items through discussion.

TIME AND LEADERSHIP

RECOGNIZE THE UNIQUENESS OF THIS RESOURCE

MANAGING TIME IS MISNOMER

PLANNING OVERCOMES PARKINSON'S LAW

PLAN, ACT, EVALUATE

BLOCK INTERRUPTIONS

GET RID OF STEREOTYPES

MAXIMIZE SUBORDINATES

STREAMLINE MEETINGS

MANAGE THE TELEPHONE

USE UNIVERSAL TIMESAVERS

ELIMINATE UNIVERSAL TIME WASTERS

HAVE A PROPER TIME ATTITUDE

EXERCISE #5

These discussion-provoking questions are designed to reinforce some information already covered on the transparencies and to build readiness for subsequent material. The exercise is placed at this point in the seminar to give variety to the presentation and to permit involvement of the group members.

Again, there are no correct answers, but responses should begin to show mastery of seminar concepts.

POWER PLOYS

MEETINGS — WHERE HELD
POWER SEATING
DEFENSES
USE OF ENVIRONMENT
WHO COMES

LIGHTING

DEFEAT ADVERSARIES, NOT SUPERIORS

SELF-EFFACEMENT

ABRASIVENESS VS. GENTLENESS

INDISPENSABILITY

BUDGET POWER

DEBT-CREATING

OFFICE ARRANGEMENT

MYSTERY-CREATING

ATTAINMENT OF TITLE

PROPAGANDA

GOSSIP

TRANSPARENCY 19

The material presented here illustrates the importance of dress to successful leadership. There is not anything particularly new or unusual, but a discussion of this sort provides a good review of information which needs to be called again to our attention.

CLOTHES, GROOMING AND LEADERSHIP

CLOTHES AND GROOMING SHOULD BE SCIENTIFICALLY DONE.

AVOID WHIM, TASTE AND SOMEONE ELSE'S REASON FOR DRESSING.

RECOGNIZE DRESS REFLECTS ENVIRONMENT:
OTHERS JUDGE US BY OUR ENVIRONMENT.

THE LOOK OF SUCCESS BRINGS RESPONSE TO SUCCESS.

DRESS AND GROOMING CAN BE USED TO CREATE IMAGES.

KEY ITEMS: SHIRT OR BLOUSE
            OVERCOAT
            DRESS OR SUIT (COLOR, FIT, STYLE)
            TIE
            SHOES

HAIRCUTS, SHAVES, BEARDS, MOUSTACHES
CLEANLINESS OF CLOTHING
SOCKS AND TIES
DEODORANTS, PERFUMES   BREATH CARE
EYEGLASSES   WATCHES
WIGS   HAIR DYES
EYEBROWS   DANDRUFF

TRANSPARENCY 20

Communication is truly crucial to successful leadership. Particular emphasis should be given to the three elements of communication, namely, the sender, the medium, and the receiver. The point should be stressed that communication really doesn't occur until the intended message has been received.

COMMUNICATION

. . . THREE BASIC ELEMENTS

SENDER $\longleftarrow$ MEDIUM $\longrightarrow$ RECEIVER

. . . SPEAK EFFECTIVELY, CONFIDENTLY, PROPERLY

. . . LISTEN EFFICIENTLY: CLARIFY BY QUESTIONING

. . . WRITE PRECISELY, BRIEFLY AND TO EXPLAIN, NOT ENTERTAIN

. . . LEARN TO HANDLE EMOTIONAL SITUATIONS IN COMMUNICA-
TION

. . . POLISH TELEPHONE SKILLS

. . . BE PREPARED FOR CONFERENCES

. . . STUDY GROUP DYNAMICS

. . . MAKE INTRODUCTIONS PROPERLY

. . . LEARN NAMES AND REMEMBER THEM

. . . STUDY BODY LANGUAGE, READ AUDIENCE REACTIONS

. . . KNOW EFFECTS OF ENVIRONMENT

. . . HOLD QUALITY MEETINGS

TRANSPARENCY 21

Job mobility within an organization and between organizations is a part of the normal experiences of a leader. This material contains the psychological and technical preparation which is necessary to get ahead. Of particular importance in the triangle for promotions, once the base of competence is achieved then visibility must be gained, normally through the use of a sponsor. A discussion of how sponsors can be attracted and visibility attained is helpful.

HARNESSING AMBITION TO GET THE JOB OR PROMOTION

AMBITION IS ESSENTIAL TO LEADERSHIP.
　　A LEADER IS PLANNING NOW FOR THE NEXT STEP UP.
THE LEADER ANNOUNCES A COURSE;
　　FOLLOWERS LET HIM PASS AND HELP HIM ALONG.

PROMOTION OR
　　A BETTER JOB
　　　　REQUIRE THREE BASIC ELEMENTS

SPONSORSHIP VISIBILITY COMPETENCE

IT IS HELPFUL TO SEEK TASKS
　　TO SHOW COMPETENCE AND GAIN VISIBILITY.
　　　　AVOID BEING PESKY BY CONSTANTLY SEEKING EVERY
　　　　OPENING OR OVERSELLING.
　　　　QUALITY IS THE KEY IN CONTACTS.
LEARN HOW TO GET YOUR HAT IN THE RING;
　　　　　　　　　EACH POSITION IS DIFFERENT.

POLISH THE RÉSUMÉ.
　　STUDY SUCCESSFUL JOB APPLICATIONS.
PREPARE FOR THE INTERVIEW BY KNOWING THE INTERVIEWER(S).
　　STUDY THE ORGANIZATION; KNOW ITS BIASES.
　　　　MAKE A POSITIVE INTERVIEW IMPRESSION BY PREPARING IN
　　　　ADVANCE.

TRANSPARENCY 22

Good leaders are responsible not only for their own activities but for the achievement of subordinates. The presentation in this transparency reviews how to assign complete jobs along with the necessary authority to complete the task.

EFFECTIVE USE OF SUBORDINATES

RAISE THEM TO THEIR LEVEL OF COMPETENCE.
ALL ARE UNDERUTILIZED.

ASSIGN TASKS IN GENERAL TERMS; LET THEM ACT INDEPENDENTLY.

EMPLOY WHOLESOME ACCOUNTABILITY.

SET REASONABLE DEADLINES AND HOLD TO THEM.
(AVOID PARKINSON'S LAW)

HELP THEM "LIVE WITH THEIR MONKEYS."

REQUIRE ORGANIZED PRESENTATIONS.

WHEN DELEGATING TO A COMMITTEE
. . . KEEP IT SMALL
. . . DEFINE TASKS
. . . USE "SELF-DESTRUCT CONCEPT"

OVERCOME STEREOTYPE OF POSITIONS
SUCH AS "SECRETARY."

TRANSPARENCY 23

This transparency contains a list which itemizes negative leadership skills. These are the things which cause us to be less effective than we could be potentially. The more of these characteristics we have, the less apt we are to be successful leaders.

NEGATIVE LEADERSHIP SKILLS

PLAYING FAVORITES

CREATOR OF ULCER ATMOSPHERE

UNPREDICTABILITY

FAILURE TO BE PUNCTUAL

PROCRASTINATION

GARBLED COMMUNICATION

INSENSITIVITY TO CO-WORKERS

POOR EXAMPLES IN DRESS

PESSIMISM

WORKAHOLISM

BLAMING OTHERS (SCAPEGOATISM)

DISORGANIZED OFFICE

PRONE TO ANGER

NO SENSE OF HUMOR

EXERCISE #6

This is a debriefing of the material contained in the entire seminar. The various parts of the activities should be done on a group basis, and sufficient time should be allowed for all participants to contribute liberally to the discussion.

Once this activity is complete, the leader should provide his perception of correct responses to the activity, and variances between his thinking and that of the group should be explored as time permits.

EXERCISE #6

1. List ten effective motivators.

   _____

   _____

   _____

   _____

   _____

2. Identify five common errors people make in attempting to get a new or better job.

   _____

   _____

   _____

   _____

3. An employee comes in for his annual evaluation conference with you. Without prior notification, he brings along a lawyer and a tape recorder. What do you, his superior, do?

   _____

   _____

   _____

   _____

   _____

4. You want to sell an idea to your boss. What do you think about, plan, and consider prior to your conference with him?

   _____

   _____

   _____

5. How would you design, furnish, and equip a leadership office?

   _____

   _____

   _____

   _____

   _____